From 1909...
Autobiography of Queen Ratnaprava Devi

From 1909...
Autobiography of Queen Ratnaprava Devi

Translation
Dr. Julie Mishra
Dr. Tapan K Panda

BLACK EAGLE BOOKS
2021

BLACK EAGLE BOOKS

USA address:
7464 Wisdom Lane
Dublin, OH 43016

India address:
E/312, Trident Galaxy, Kalinga Nagar,
Bhubaneswar-751003, Odisha, India

E-mail: info@blackeaglebooks.org
Website: www.blackeaglebooks.org

Original Book Published in Odiya by Rajeev Lochan Singh Deo
Bidyut Marg 9(1) Bhubaneswar
First Published – Dussehra -1997

First International Edition Published by
BLACK EAGLE BOOKS, 2021

AUTOBIOGRAPHY OF QUEEN RATNAPRAVA DEVI
Translation **Dr. Julie Mishra, Dr. Tapan K Panda**

Original Copyright © **Brig. Kamakhya Prasad Singh Deo**
Translation Copyright © **Dr. Julie Mishra, Dr. Tapan K Panda**

All rights reserved. No part of this publication may be reproduced, stored in a retrieval system, or transmitted, in any form or by any means, electronic, mechanical, photocopying, recording or otherwise without the prior permission of the publisher.

Cover & Interior Design: Ezy's Publication

ISBN- 978-1-64560-180-7 (Paperback)
Library of Congress Control Number: 2021936561

Printed in United States of America

Rajmata Ratnaprava Devi
Birth: December 1909 (Margashira Krushna Chaturdarshi)

Marriage: 1924

Member of Orissa Legislative Assembly
1956- 1971

PREFACE

BHUBANESWAR, JUNE 12 1995
Bidyut Marg 9 (1)

Om Namo Bhagavate Vasudevaya
Hari Om

Almost two years back when I visited Delhi, my elder son Kamakhya, once told me, "Mother! In the old age a person loses temper along with some level of memory power, therefore whatever you contemplate, transcribe them in the form of a book". Since then I started writing this autobiography, which is entwined with 70 years of old, sweet and bitter memories of mine in Dhenkanal. The readers will acquire some general knowledge from whatever is written in this book. I have written the book according to my convenience and time; so it may lack the continuity of the events and therefore I am begging pardon from my readers.

I don't carry an assumption that I am a pundit. If the readers are able to acquire some values and prudence from my book and show their reverence towards me, my writing will be meaningful.

Ratna Prava Devi
1997

A FEW LINES

Shri Sesha Prasad Singh Deo

I am obliged as I got a chance to write a few lines regarding this book.
Almost 70 years back, during the monarchy of the ruler, leaving behind the Purda system, Rani Ratna Prava Devi, motivated the villagers to go to the hospital for treatment. After achieving success in this movement she formed the Girl Guide taking the villagers into confidence. She was the chief guide of this Girl Guide party. She could influence others by branching out this organization in various cities like Delhi, Bombay etc.
She has acquired a lot of knowledge about western culture on her visit to different countries like England, Scotland, South and Middle Europe, North America, and Canada.
She was the head of Dhenkanal's endowment department and I worked according to her instructions as an endowment officer. Unlike today, the work regulated by the endowment department of those days wasn't unplanned and chaotic.
She was elected thrice as the representative of Odisha Legislative Assembly from 1956 to 1971 in independent India.
She is a pious lady; worshipped many gods and

goddesses to be blessed with children. As the pride and prestige of the nation, her elder son Kamakhya Prasad SinghDeo is the minister of Information and Technology in the union ministry.

This memoir written by her isn't the first Odiya book by her. Her first Odiya book was 'Girl Guide Sikhya'. This book is listed in the catalogue of many renowned booksellers.

I hope that this book also will be appreciated by the readers and will enrich Odiya literature.

Boraapada **Shri Sesha Prasad SinghDeo**
Dhenkanal, (Awarded by Odiya Sahitya Academy)
30/06/95

FOREWORD

Brigadier Kamakhya Prasad SinghDeo
Dhenkanal

MAA

MAA is the first word uttered by any child and I am no exception. My Maa Ratna Prava used to tell me how, for seventeen years she longed to be addressed as such from a child born from her womb. Though she didn't have any children of her own she embraced all children of Dhenkanal, who addressed her as "Maa Agyan".

World-renowned gynecologists from Rockefeller Institute, New York, Col. Green Armitage from London, Vienna, Dr. Mudaliar from Madras and Dr. Subodh Mitra from Calcutta, who operated on her, opinioned that, she would not or could not ever bear a child. So my father Shankar Pratap gave her permission by an adoption deed in 1939 to adopt a son. But the Political Department of Government of India and the Crown Representative refused to honor the deed. My father- crestfallen and humiliated rather considered abdicating the throne in favor of one of his brothers.

Maa never gave up hope and faith in GOD and her self-determination. Like a commander preparing for war, she persevered, prayed patiently, painstakingly, stoically, cheerfully in her "Selection and Maintenance of Aim" in begetting a child, by concentrating all her faculties – body, mind and soul through severe penance, prayers, meditations, sacrifices, pilgrimages selflessly and courageously- thus ultimately succeeded in invoking the blessings of GOD – "MAA KAMAKHYA" and bore two children namely Kamakhya Prasad and Matru Prasad.

'Yatho Dharma Sthatho Jay'.

In her quest for begetting a child and fulfilling the aspirations of any mother, anywhere in the universe, MAA Ratna Prava immersed herself in learning, studying, reading, carrying out duties, responsibilities and obligations as per social customs, practice, traditions, ethics and ethos prevalent in family, society and state to finally assimilate herself as an embodiment of mother to all.

In 1943 November, when I was two years& three months old, my baby brother had been born, my father wrote me a letter, containing a number of articles on various subjects. Among the subjects was a chapter on GOD. In this chapter he concludes, "YOUR LIVING GOD IS YOUR MOTHER, DEAR CHILD" and your place is "ALWAYS AT HER FEET".

So what can I say and recall about My GOD my MAA.

"Everything about My GOD was Beautiful, Graceful,

Cheerful, Smiling, Serene, Calm, Composed, Loving, Affectionate, Caring, Sweet, Firm, Polite, Kind, Considerate". I could run up to her for shelter, confide, seek advice, guidance and direction, unburden all my woes and confusion and she would light a path for me to follow as a way out of the trouble, a simple solution to the most complicated situations with intensity and sincerity. She would emphasize and command respect to women, aged, scholars, saints and Brahmins, affection and concern for lesser fortunate members of society, kindness to children, animals, birds and creatures.

Her passion was for the upliftment, empowerment and improvement of dignity, self-respect of women and the girl child, health care and maternity care. Girl guiding, knitting, childcare, first aid were various mediums used by her to achieve these goals. Social Welfare, Religious Discourse, efficient management of religious institutions and building Community Life through development were her other passions.

She liked to be surrounded by people, family, friends and children in her happy contented God ordained Life's long journey.

I am proud to say SHE WAS MY GOD AND MY MOTHER.

I AM ALWAYS AT YOUR FEET TO DO THY WISH AND BIDDING WITH YOUR BLESSINGS I SHALL CONTINUE TO LIVE UP TO YOUR EXPECTATIONS.

(BRIG. KAMAKHYA PRASAD SINGH DEO)

The Story of Love, Courage and Valour

It has been more than two years since we met Brigadier Kamakhya Prasad Singh Deo- The current king of Dhenkanal and royal family in Dhenkanal palace. It was possible due to our dear friend, well known exponent of Odiya culture and tourism Sri Manoj Bhoi. Often Manoj will bring in the history and saga of Dhenkanal Kingdom in our conversations. Like many Odiya people, we had also much confusion and misunderstanding about Dhenkanal palace and its kings. There is no harm in accepting the fact that we were a bit hesitant to meet them- kings have their own way of handling people isn't it!

But we were proven wrong. We were scheduled to spend half an hour in the palace for a just conversation but as we remember, the conversation went for hours together. The king Brigadier Kamakhya Prasad Singh Deo is a successful and nationally well-known Odiya politician who has been elected multiple times to Parliament and was also a minister in the central government. The aura of being a king and a successful politician made us a bit hesitant to start the conversation. But to our surprise, the king was kind enough to take us through his life journey; in between the queen and princess also joined us. The prince Amarjyoti was not in the palace, so we missed him on that day.

One thing that struck us during our conversation was the love for the Queen Mother Late Ratnaprava Devi. Significant part of Odisha history was written in the Dhenkanal palace which had witnessed the visit and meetings of many leaders including Late Biju Pattnaik, Late Rajendra Narayan Singh Deo and many more. Late King Shankar Pratap Singh Deo was part of Rajya Sabha (Upper House) and had an untimely death while Late Ratna Prava Devi was a member of Odisha Legislative Assembly from 1956 to 1971.

After rounds of tea cups and snacks and visits to a number of albums available with the royal family made us feel the love and affection they carried for common people like us. We discovered the existence of this book (From 1909...) during our conversation. The late queen mother wrote this book in 1999 when she was 84 years old. Subsequently Manoj was able to spare a copy of the book with me. I guess he had a copy only. The king was kind enough to allow us to translate the book into English and agreed to write a foreword for the English version.

The lock down helped me (Tapan) a lot to start writing, translating and composing again. I was postponing the creative pursuit as I was busy with my academic and research career. The pressure from large clients ruled over my time as a brand consultant and I postponed doing any serious work for almost two decades.

I started reading the book; making notes; discussing with Julie (as she is a Political Science Faculty) about the subject matter. Then one day, I concluded that this work is not my cup of tea as there were so many terms, words and concepts involved in the autobiography that needed additional knowledge on politics, sociology and history. So Julie joined the project and played a big role in translating the gazette and other official documents of Dhenkanal estate.

We also wish to thank Sri Bibek Mishra, another tourism and travel expert and elder brother for accessing the photos from the family album. We wish to thank Sri Satya Pattanaik, publisher, BlackEagle Books to take the responsibility of bringing out this edition. In our later conversation, we were pleased to know that his father Late Sri Harekrishna Pattnaik had acquaintances with the queen mother as he hails from Saptasajya of Dhenkanal.

The content of this book is part of Odisha history. We were proud to read that Netaji had escaped from British captive in Kolkata in the estate car of late King Shankar Pratap Singh Deo- maybe the king was paying back for the care he got as a small child from Netaji's father Late Janaki Bose. One can also read how the foundation of grass root governance was set up in the Dhenkanal estate through enactment of Village Panchayat or Union published in the estate gazette.

Translation is a very difficult task as it can either be beautiful or honest. For an autobiography and socio-political commentary like this, we decided to be honest- so we owe all the flaws in this book. We are sure this book is going to be an important document on the modern political history of Odisha.

Dr Julie Mishra
Dr Tapan K Panda

CHAPTERS

Chapter-1 From the Year 1909 till Present	21
Chapter-II Birth of Brilliant and Propitious Shura Pratap	25
Chapter-III My Childhood and Seraikela's History and Heritage	39
Chapter-IV Dhenkanal during My Marriage	48
Chapter-V Dhenkanal's Royal Family & Its Administration	113
Post Script-1 Baji Rout	131
Post Script-2 My Family Life	134
Annexure- 1- Constitution of the Council	136
Annexure-II- Darabar's Address –Dhenkanal	146
Annexure-3- Proclamation	156
Annexure-4- Constitution of Village Panchayat...	159
Annexure-5- Dhenkanal State Gazette- Declaration...	169
Annexure-6- Notes written by Raja Shankar Pratap...	171
Annexure-7- On the Pious Day of Jesus Birth	175
Annexure-8- Death of Dhenkanal King	176
Annexure-9- Viceroy's Agent	183

Chapter-1

FROM THE YEAR 1909 TILL PRESENT

I am now 84 years old. I came to Dhenkanal in the year 1924. From my personal experience of 70 years in Dhenkanal, I am writing this for the sake of my children. Though I am aged, still my mind and body are hale and hearty. Therefore I don't feel the frailty of my old age, other than that the joyful world in the presence of my two competent sons, grandson, granddaughter, great- grandson and great- granddaughter always enthuse me to lead a divine life.

At present also there is no sign of squalidity in my thoughts and deeds. The incidents that happened in these 84 years, many self-redeemed stories, various situations and the operational events come to my conscious mind in essence. They aren't only memorable but also edifying and delightful. The recollection of these thousand memories weaves the thread into the woof and invigorates my decrepit frame. When I feel lonesome in this long sojourn, I remember my adorable soul mate Honorary Wing Commander King Shankar Pratap Singh Deo Mahendra Bahadur Vidyasagar FRAS (Fellow of Royal Asiatic Society) True Massonic Lodge, Scotland Yard, Magic Circle, London, Diploma from Berlitz School of Language, Berlin.

King Shankar Pratap was an idealistic and godlike human being. He had a simple lifestyle. He was a man of wisdom and modesty. During judicial discussions, he very keenly observed and analyzed each minute detail. He picked up the truth and edged forward with it. He had a deep abhorrence towards falsehood. He could immediately recognize the people telling lies and kept himself away from them. He never gave an opportunity to people who impersonate. That's why many mendacious and impersonate people to accomplish their self-interest weaved delusion and became mischief- makers as a part of historical conspiracy. He understood how people got carried away by these allurers; still, he never did any harm to them. He was a symbol of generosity and forgiveness. He handled the debacle himself and secured others. He had abundant knowledge in Science, Literature, Arts, History, Geography, Biology, Zoology and Science of warfare. He was a voracious reader and read many books to acquire knowledge about various issues. His only hobby was to purchase various books and to read.

He read the books so attentively that he could remember the count, page, and the content without much difficulty. He had a sharp memory. He tried to implement the knowledge that he gained from the books and the knowledge that he acquired about art and culture from his travel to various places in India and abroad in his state to refine the conduct and to enlighten the people.

His foremost concern was, how will the general public of Dhenkanal acquire dignity because of the knowledge, will be revered and victorious. It was always in his thought process and he worked for it according to his potential. He wrote the summary of all the books distinctly with very beautiful handwriting before the first page with the apprehension that maybe someone won't be able to read it completely or he may forget the content of the book. Reading the summary itself reflected the content of the book and gave a feeling as if someone has read the entire content. It was another aspect of his knowledge. He didn't take the help of anyone to keep the books safely rather he stitched the books properly, bound them, and kept them intact.

The qualities which a successful man has like virtue, nobility and erudition were found in him. Those who have got an opportunity to mingle with him can freely, without any hesitation accept this. At present many of them who are placed in a dignified position also acknowledged that he was a brilliant and gifted personality. He was an epitome of a successful and eminent person and in total the happiest, prosperous, and glorified soul.

He was a devout person. He not only visited the religious institutions and offered his prayer piously in the state and the country but also strictly adhered to the norms and regulations of the pious institutions. He visited all the deities in Odisha and other than that visited the deities and pious places like Amarnath, Kedarnath, Badrinath, Kanykumari, Rameshwaram, Kamakhya and Padmanava Swami, Natraj, Pakhitirtha, Shri Lanka, and Dhaka .

He took the advantage of offering prayer at the pilgrimage and also to visit various places with scenic beauty because of this he could contemplate the history, art, culture, heritage, language, education etc and latched on to the essence of it to implement it in projects. He could mingle with people very easily. He never discriminated against people according to their wealth, education, or status in society. He accepted the positive aspects of other countries irrespective of religion, caste, and creed. Apart from India, he visited the countries like England, The United States of

America, Hungary, Yugoslavia, Germany, France, Egypt, Austria, Scotland etc like a true Indian keeping his self-esteem intact along with his family.

During our visit to foreign countries he always kept in mind the culture and heritage of our country and worked accordingly because of this he was appreciated and revered even in a foreign land. At that time it was a pride for our country. It was not a trivial thing as at that time the people of the ruling country revered a person who belonged to the ruled country. He was able to capture the attention of others for his ability and talent. He emerged as a brilliant and gifted personality which caught the attention of many envious people. He was steady, intellectual and never showed abhorrence towards anyone. He had an ever bright multifaceted personality.

He was devoted to his parents. His father Late king Shura Pratap Mahendra Bahadur was a godly man. He ruled over his kingdom with religiousness, righteousness, truthfulness, and mercifulness and it's regarded as the brightest period in history. Whoever has come in contact with him can never forget him and his pleasant memories. He died at the age of 33 in the year 1918 while working for the benefit and prosperity of his kingdom. Shankar Pratap was only 14 years old at that time. Though he was an innocent child, he was influenced by his father's reasoning and intelligence. He wasn't shattered by his father's untimely demise but overcame the grief with a lot of patience and perseverance. He sometimes wondered whether he could repay the debt towards his father during his lifetime and fixed his goal and duty in that melancholy.

Chapter-2

BIRTH OF BRILLIANT AND PROPITIOUS SHURA PRATAP

In the year 1885 on the day of Shivaratri when Lord Chandrashekhar's Maha Deepa was lightened on that auspicious moment, Rajashree Shura Pratap was born. His birth time gave him a place of divinity. His mother means late my grandmother- in- law Annapurna Devi was an intelligent, pious woman and was accomplished with all the virtues. She nurtured her only son Shura Pratap with all her exceptional qualities. King Shura Pratap spent his short- lived life working for the progress of his subjects, visiting pilgrimage and in worshiping the deities. He took diksha from the priest Late Madhusudan Goswami of Shri Radha Raman Jew temple at Vrindaban and spent his life like a true saint working for the benefit of his subjects.

King Shura Pratap did all the arrangements for the worship in the Kunjakanta temple after its construction. He constructed a rest house for the pilgrims near Kapilash's Chandrasekhar temple. From Deogao till the temple he lay the road which was much appreciated. His mother installed the deity of Narayan in the temple under his supervision. Under his supervision, the deity was sculptured in such a way that the spring water of Kapilash seemed to be flowing from the feet of the deity which enthralled the devotees and filled their heart with devotion. Kapilash is a historical pilgrimage with abundant scenic beauty. All the sorrows and grief of life vanishes when a person visits this place and worship Lord Chandrashekhar and witness the beauty of nature which nature has benevolently bestowed in this place. The rippling, bubbling of the spring, the chirping of birds, the sight of the leaping monkeys, and the gentle touch of the breeze cart-off the anguish and pain.

King Shura Pratap Mahendra Bahadur tried to establish a college along with Dhenkanal High School. During the construction of the High School, he died and the construction work was stopped. Later on to complete his incomplete work his son King Shankar Pratap tried his best. Because of uncertainty in the state and for few selfish and mischievous people he couldn't succeed. Still he tried his best and waited for a favorable situation to complete it.

My father the King of Sareikela Late Aditya Pratap Singh Deo and my reverend father- in- law were relatives as they were brother in laws. My aunt Krushna Chandra Priya was married to Shura Pratap Mahendra Bahadur. During his death, my father came to Dhenkanal to console his sister and nephews. After the last rite was performed my father was handed over a piece of paper to read which was handwritten by King Shura Pratap. It was mentioned in the paper regarding the distribution of the barn among his five sons for their maintenance.

After reading the piece of paper his elder nephew returned the piece of paper to Shankar Pratap without commenting over it. It was a clear indication to perform the responsibility with devotion. Shankar Pratap kept this small piece of paper securely so that when the right time comes he can do the necessary according to his father's instructions. When he became a major and governed his state, according to his father's instruction he legally transferred the landed property and the barns in the name of his brothers. In this way, he obediently stuck to his father's instruction and did his duty towards his minor brothers. He had lots of love and affection towards his younger brothers and his brothers also reciprocated in the similar manner.

He was determined to give them good educational facilities and to establish them as good human beings. He always insisted them to be self reliant. His younger brother Late Shri Nursingha Pratap SinghDeo was sent to England to study Bar At Law. His third brother Prince Shri Shrisesh Pratap SinghDeo was sent to Cuttack to complete his Bachelor's degree and was later sent to Patna to study law. His fourth brother Shri Brajesh Pratap Singh Deo was made the king of Damapada. At Damapada he began his reign as Amarendra Mansigh Bhramarabara Ray. He faced a lot of problems regarding this and had to approach Previ Council for a solution to this. He own the case there. He sent his fifth and the sixth brothers Gourendra Pratap SinghDeo and Samarendra Pratap SinghDeo to Leeds University and Kings College, London University for further studies respectively.

Shri Gourendra represented International Hockey from England and in the year 1934 he along with Pandit Bamadeba Rath, IAS and Flg. Officer Binay Ghosh, IAS represented in Australia from World Scout Jombree. He motivated Shri Samarendra to appear for Indian Police(IP) examination and he came out in flying colors. At that time, in Odisha only a handful of people were appointed as a high rank official in the police department. He was appointed at Munger as Police Superintendent but he refused the offer as he had to work for the Britishers. King Shankar Pratap not only thought about the academic achievement of his brothers but also took the initiative to help the poor and brilliant students of Dhenkanal.

He had also sent a few of them to England and other foreign countries for higher education. Among them were Late Pandit Sekhreswar Mishra, Late Pandit Bamadeba Rath, Shri Harekrushna Mishra, Shri Banchanidhi Mishra, Shri Rama Krushna Mangaraj, Shri Krushna Chandra Harichandan Singh, and many more. He had sent Abhaya Shankar Ray and Ajay Shankar Ray to Japan and Germany respectively to study about cottage industry, food technology, and art and printing. He lend a helping hand to send S.P Burman, son of S.P Rai Bahadur Shri Brajbihari Burman to England to complete Bar At Law. Later on, S.P Burman became the Chief Justice in Odisha High Court.

The most appreciated quality of his was, he didn't keep any property in his name. Few of his relatives and his well-wishers advised him to keep few barns in his name but he refused to do so. His arguments and justification regarding this were strong and it reflected his spirituality. His justification was, "I am only a mere human being. My fate is not in my hands. A man is born with empty hands and will leave this world with empty hands".

He sometimes asked, "Future will take care of itself." What is the necessity of thinking today about tomorrow? This question made people keep their mouths shut. The enlightened consciousness of his always initiated him to do his duty whole heartedly. He was never attracted to money, jewelry, and property. Greed could never take him in its clutches. He kept himself away from money and thought that property and money is the root cause of all the disasters.

My father in law King Shura Pratap was interested in psalmody and havan .In a similar way my husband also had those noble virtues. At that time he invited the renowned psalmodist Ramdas Babuji many a time to perform Asta Prahari and Chabis Prahari. He invited the famous Bhagabat Gita Pandit Kuluda Bhusan Mallik and many more wise spiritual people to give a discourse on Bhagabat Gita and Purana. He arranged for Nama Sankirtana every Sunday evening and the objective behind it was to motivate others to attain spirituality in this busy and mundane life. He acquired a lot of strength from these rituals and made himself unconquerable. Sometimes he arranged meetings to discuss on Rasaleela, Ramayana, and Mahabharata and keenly studied all the elements of it and pursued it in his life. He was truly spiritual and piety. To promote Nama Sankirtana and spirituality he had appointed two people to supervise psalmody in Dhenkanal and Madhi (which was named as Kamakhya Nagar on the first birthday of Kamakhya Prasad on 9th August 1942).

For the betterment of education in villages, agriculture, health, forest protection, to sort out the disputes and to initiate spirituality he established assembly house and Bhagabata house in the villages which were one of his envisage. All of them gathered there to discuss regarding the management in the village and after the discussion Purana was read and Nama Sankirtana was done frequently. This was effective for leading a spiritual life, to maintain law and order, and to do the duty faithfully. The values helped him to live a disciplined and peaceful life throughout his life despite of the riches.

As he led a disciplined and peaceful life he also motivated others in this regard. After reading the newly published police manual, he always thought, how everyone will follow a disciplined life, how will they be devoted to their duties, how will they do regular exercise to keep themselves fit and lead a harmonious life. Because of that he sincerely started the program 'Boy Scout' and 'Girl Scout' in his state. He was not only contented with the training, rather he thought, because of this program how Dhenkanal will achieve the top rank and be praiseworthy. So he encouraged the people accordingly. He took strong steps so that Dhenkanal will emerge as an unparalleled estate.

Under my leadership, the girl guides participated in an event in Calcutta and were appreciated. It was in the year 1935, the girls who never stepped out of their house performed in the presence of many people. Taking them to Calcutta which is a very big city and to make them participate in an event wasn't a small matter for us. On that day the people of Calcutta appreciated the performance of the Girl Guide of Dhenkanal. Lord Bedane Pauale and his wife Lady Baden Pauale appreciated and encouraged us. They proclaimed that the scouting and Girl Guide program has been appreciated all over the world and the contribution of Dhenkanal is much appreciated.

Because of this praiseworthy role of Girl Guide, Dhenkanal's Girl Guide group participated in the Scout and Guide Jambori meet in Holland and was acknowledged. Lady Pauale was fascinated by our Girl Guide program and recommended our Girl Guide to participate in various programs. She recommended us to visit America's Scouting and Girl Guide's main office and Washington. We visited and came to know about various aspects of Girl Guide program. The king rescued the children from the blazing hut and was awarded the highest award of scouting 'Silver Cross'. I pay my homage to the late king who was influenced by the love, affection, and sincerity of Lord Baden Pauale and Lady Baden Pauale. They were true worshippers of talent. They always encouraged us for our devotion towards work and for our inner strength. King Shankar Pratap wasn't only happy for this achievement but also was happy for all the achievements of Dhenkanal in various aspects.

My friend, Doctor Smt. D.M Leslie helped me in my work. She was a hard working, knowledgeable, and virtuous lady. She taught me, French. At that time those who knew French were regarded highly. I could speak French fluently because of her. King Shankar Pratap took his diploma from Germany's Berlitz School that's why during our tour to western countries we didn't face any difficulties rather our dignity was enhanced. I remember Smt. Leslie and pay my homage to her.

The lady doctor of Dhenkanal Smt. R.K Bodhak looked after the hospital work and with my inspiration participated in the women welfare program and also organized many programs successfully. Her contribution to Girl Guide program is immense.

Along with the regular course offered to students in the school, King Shankar Pratap looked after sports, exercise, and gardening. Other than that he tried to include farming, gardening, and forest- related topics in the curriculum to make it skill- based education. Right from childhood, each student should have an interest in farming, children shouldn't be alienated towards their work was his fundamental purpose. He tried to shape the students into good human beings not only by direction and instruction but also by appropriate training. He was realistic in this regard. I can give an example to make it clearer. When our elder son Shreeman Kamakhya Prasad was 3-4 years old child, Subedar Shyam Singh, Habildar Ramakrushna

Mangaraj, Inspector Govind Chandra ,Shri Chandan Rai , and Habildar Naulakha Singh were appointed to teach him to parade, horse riding and physical exercises. At that time we didn't like this. When it was told that it's not necessary to give such difficult training to a child, he didn't agree to it. The training continued under his strict supervision.

During the parade sometimes he was present in person or kept an eye on the training without anyone's knowledge. He gave rigid instructions to the appointed instructors to rectify even small mistakes. As a result of this training, Shri Kamakhya Prasad, later on, joined India's Territorial Army. He fought against Pakistan in the year 1971 for the Indo Pak war and in 1976 he was the commander of the Territorial Army in the Republic Day parade. During the training when Naulakha Singh became a little liberal, he wasn't spared. King Shankar Pratap inferred from his experience that if the quality of education isn't up to the mark if the teacher becomes liberal during imparting education and the student doesn't reciprocate well to the education imparted then life becomes despondent later on.

During his lifetime whatever suggestions and instructions he had given were very fruitful in life. Those who were associated with him could perceive it. Shriman Kamakhya implemented his father's suggestions and instructions in his life and carried on the training and could be disciplined and successful. Though his father isn't alive today his soul must be at peace looking at his son's success.

I still visit different places in the country regarding various works and at various places, I hear from the people regarding Kamakhya's popularity and work ethics and we take the pride in that. He has received the appropriate training from his father and could mold his life accordingly.

He has given shape to a multifaceted personality within him and could exhibit his ability in various fields to gain recognition and respect. He had helped people according to his capability and had earned his name and fame. He firmly upholds his father's advice, ideology, and strategy.

Without expecting anything in return from the people he has rendered his services to get eternal peace. As a patriot, he joined the Territorial Army, fought in Indo Pak war, and brought laurels to Dhenkanal. I feel that it's the greatest pride for a mother like me. It was only possible because of his father's training and guidance. Shriman Kamakhya is simple, calm, benevolent, patient, and considerate. He is a down to earth person with a very simple lifestyle but he is bold, a Good Samaritan, and jovial. He is highly intellectual. He slowly and steadily picked up all these lessons from his father. Not only Kamakhya but also those who followed King Shankar Pratap's footsteps have achieved success in life. There are so many examples like this. Many people who are still alive, who remember him pay their tribute to him.

At that time King Shankar Pratap went to the nearby villages to inspect the adult education centers and the Scouting program. Other than these he made a surprise visit to the police station, school, and range office. He also visited the villages to check the undertakings. This enthused people. Any mistakes committed in the work were immediately reformed and those who were recognized as skilled were appreciated in various ways. Sometimes in our presence camp firing was conducted and the villagers equally participated in this.

As we attended these programs, the villagers were happy and enthusiastic and as a result, the program was a success. There was no chance of duping as all of them were interested in these progress- oriented programs. The education system was also good at Dhenkanal. At present other than general education and vocational education government has started adult education and complete literacy programs. Almost 50 to 60 years back the villagers along with all the employees of the king's court were involved in the enhancement of education. The villagers contributed not only in the field of education but also in other fields like farming, health etc. according to their capability. That's the reason why chaos couldn't reign, the moral value was intact and falsehood couldn't spread its fangs in the society or in the administration of the state. The number of illiterate people in Dhenkanal was very less compared to Mugalbadi and other states.

Dhenkanal acquired a good reputation and was glorified. As good education was imparted to the people of Dhenkanal, so they were submissive, courteous, and diligent. They were devoid of false vanity. They never neglected their work nor duped .They showed care and conscientiousness towards their work or duties. They were virtuous and uncomplicated therefore at many times the people of Mugalbadi used offensive language and ridiculed them. But the people of Dhenkanal never paid attention to this. They thought that using offensive language and ridiculing others is the characteristic of an irrational person and they are away from this because of their education, thought process, and conduct." Namranti phalino vrikshah Namranti gunino janah".

This is the characteristic of the people of Dhenkanal. They were empowered with knowledge, virtue, courtesy, diligence, selflessness, and benevolence as they were born in the land of Dhenkanal. Those who addressed them as 'Dhenkanaliya' and mocked them only revealed their narrow mindset, impoliteness, and indecent behavior. The people of Dhenkanal take pride in being addressed as 'Dhenkanaliya' because they are virtuous and they have acquired the top positions in the state administration .It's high time now. If the people can follow the rules and regulations followed during our time then the present society which is on the verge of collapsing can be retrieved. The country will prosper and people will be free from the shackles of prejudice and lead a happy and prosperous life.

Generally, royal families adhere to the norms and follow the age- old tradition. The womenfolk of royal families are bound to strict tradition and follow the Parada system. But my husband King Late Shankar Pratap was progressive, disciplined, and avant-garde. He encouraged and trained me to participate in the government work, games, scouting, and Girl Guide program. He also encouraged me to carry on my work fearlessly. It boosted my confidence and I was able to complete the assigned work flawlessly. I was also benefitted from it. The things which I achieved in my life are his benefaction and I accept it wholeheartedly.

My knowledge expanded because of him. His aim was 'Total development'. We were inspired by his thoughts and acquired them. During a few programs like Girl Guide, scouting, and games we involved our self with the common man according to his instructions to bridge the gap between us. He inspired us to be courteous and rightful. His inspiration and encouragement made me capable of achieving success in every field of work and to earn admiration. I gained the confidence to give the speech and to participate in the award distribution ceremony at Dhenkanal, Sambalpur, Pyarimohan Academy High School at Cuttack, Ravenshaw Collegiate School in the year 1926, and Ravenshaw College in the year 1928. Though I delivered a very short speech it was appropriate for the prevailing situation.

At that time I had listened to the speech of many renowned people, educationists, legal practitioners, and social workers. His dream was to mold me in such a way that I can work as a catalyst for the development of Dhenkanal. At a young age, fearlessly delivering the speech and distributing awards in Ravenshaw College amidst the highly knowledgeable teachers, high profile government servants, elderly and educated parents was only possible because of his guidance and training. Later on, when I was elected as the people's representative and represented various issues related to common people in Vidhan Sabha for the benefit of people, I could realize my husband's contribution in molding me. His endeavor, reverence, and devotion worked as a driving force for my achievements. I can never forget throughout my life the appreciation, affection and respect that I earned from all.

He was farsighted. He could visualize the future according to the present situation and be able to predict the future. His analysis was precise. For the inspirative programs in future, his vision was prudent. Taking over the reign after his father Late Shura Pratap Mahendra Bahadur's demise, he thought of developing Dhenkanal as a planned and progressive town. His first attempt was to lay wide and concrete roads and plant trees near the roadside.

He planned to lay wide roads in the lanes and by-lanes and to make a proper drainage system other than that to stop house fire was his other effort. As these plans were for the betterment of the town and for the convenience of the people so it was expected that it will be appreciated by people. While implementing the plans it was ordered by the king that no poor people should incur any loss, face any problem, and remain dissatisfied. The plans were scrutinized thoroughly and it was deduced that a poor man or general public will not incur any great loss. Hardly 3 to 4 families who had more land in the town and had acres and acres of land outside the town for cultivation purposes, some of their lands were taken to construct roads according to the rules and regulations.

Rest was left for these families for their living and they were compensated with some other land and money according to that time's current price. The roads which were laid at that time as per the planning still exist. It was an ill fate that good work wasn't appreciated. At that time the land which was taken from those 3 to 4 affluent families, cleverly resorted to falsehood and anti-propaganda which resulted in the discontinuance of the project. Even the common man believed them. No one thought about the future as a result the king's court didn't take any interest in doing any developmental work.

There wasn't enough money available and there was no chance of getting any financial help from the British government who rather extracted money from the states on some or the other pretexts. So it was decided that there won't be any such developmental programs that will create unnecessary trouble. The way there is development in the field of politics, finance and social aspects at present, considering that as a yard stick it can never be assessed that how it was against people, immoral and unjust at that time.

In the near past, the elected government demolished thousands of houses of the poor people and bereft them of their house and the source of income. No one can forget the time when the emergency was declared in the country. People lost their house, their family and also there was a lot of violence .The situation was worse than the situation during British rule. No one protested in fear. During the emergency, people realized that protest won't bear any fruit as there is no one to listen to them. There were many politicians from different parts of the country, there was an improvement in the education system and people were literate, still no one protested against the tyranny.

At present, the government acquires the land of the people at any price, at any time. In this situation, though people go to the court, spend a lot of money to seek justice but they fail to get it. The common people suffer a lot and there is no one to listen to their plight. It seems as if the society is encroached by lawlessness and standing on a foundation that will be shattered at any time. It was not so at that time. The king, the ruler, and the people who were ruled had the fear of falsehood, law, discipline and duty. Foremost they all had the fear of God the Almighty. The complaint was heard, judged and according to that a person was punished or rewarded. At that time lacuna existed but it was sorted out by reasoning. There was harmony in the relationship because of deep faith and conviction.

Chapter-III

MY CHILDHOOD- SERAIKELA'S HISTORY AND HERITAGE

I was born in Seraikela's royal family in the year 1909. At that time my father's grandfather Maharaja Udit Narayan Singh Deo was the ruler. When he was alive his son Tikayat NrupaRaj Singh Deo died and my father was made to sit on the throne. My father was the king of Seraikela. Late Aditya Pratap Singh Deo had two brothers Late Bijaya Pratap Singh Deo and Late Ajay Pratap Singh Deo. He also had three sisters. Princess of Patna State Late Padmini Kumari was my mother. We were together 6 brothers and 3 sisters. The eldest among the brothers was Late Nupendra Narayan Singh Deo. The others were Rajendra Narayan Singh Deo, Bhupendra Narayan Singh Deo, Subhendra Narayan Singh Deo, Brajendra Narayan Singh Deo, and Sudhendra Narayan Singh Deo. At present, two of my brothers Bhupendra and Subhendra are alive. Rajendra Narayan Singh Deo went to Bolangir Patana as an adopted son and occupied the royal throne.

After the Independence, he joined an independent party and was known all over India as a progressive leader. He was elected as the opposition leader in Vidhan Sabha for many years and ruled the state once as the Chief Minister.

He could establish himself as a historical man. Among the sisters, I was the eldest one. My second sister Hema Prabha got married to Patiala Maharaja Jadabendra Singh and the youngest sister Mani Prava got married to the king of Manjusha Jagannath Raj Rajmani. She had three sons and three daughters. The elder son was Colonel Chatrapati Singh Deo who was in the Indian Army and fought in Bangladesh Liberation War.

I was married to the king of Dhenkanal Shankar Pratap Singh Deo Mahendra Bahadur in the year 1924. He was my elder aunt Queen Krushna Chandra Priya and Late King Shura Pratap's elder son. My aunt was a poetess, she was intelligent and spiritual. I still remember an incident which I would like to mention. I think it was destined. I went to Puri to my aunt for Jagannath darshan. I was very small at that time. My uncle Shura Pratap was a pious, industrious, righteous, virtuous, merciful, idealistic, affectionate, truthful, calm, and poised person. He became very happy to see us and took me on his lap affectionately and said overwhelmingly, "If I make this doll my daughter-in- law then the palace will become a happy place to live in. What do you say, my friend?"

He looked at my father and asked emotionally. My aunt, uncle, father, and others who were present there laughed. As I was very young at that time so I couldn't understand anything. But after his death when his son Shankar Pratap's marriage proposal was considered, at that time my father and aunt couldn't ignore my uncle's desire. To fulfil the desire of my uncle and to pay him respect my marriage was performed in a grand ceremony. According to social norms though many questions were raised regarding this marriage finally it was accepted as it was solemnized to pay respect to my uncle's desire. We received the blessings of my father- in- law and despite of the problems we could achieve marital bliss. We could perceive his blessings and could lead a meaningful life.

My family was happy during my childhood. The people of Seraikela had a lot of love and affection for the royal family and similarly the royal family was sentimental towards its subjects. All of them had extreme faith in each other. The royal family of Seraikela was disciplined that's why there were peace and tranquillity everywhere. A very conducive atmosphere was created by the amalgamation of wise and intellectual people. We were brought up in a peaceful and tranquil atmosphere and this laid a foundation for our future. At present when I think, I could realize that I could achieve success because of the foundation which was laid in my childhood.

My mother was a very wise lady and all her work was idealistic.

She appreciated when we behaved properly and also followed strict regimentation when we were at fault. She was very good at sports and encouraged us to participate in sports and do exercise to build up stamina. She always encouraged us to read scriptures other than our regular textbooks. She also taught us how to face a difficult situation in life boldly and patiently. My mother was a virtuous lady. Her goodness and virtuousness had a deep impact on me and my siblings. All of us were able to establish ourselves in our respective domains. The blessing of our mother was the base of it. She was very vigilant regarding traditional nobility, family decorum, decision, and personal respect but still, we had personal freedom and enjoyed it under the guidance and supervision of our mother. There were no obstacles or hindrances in life. Our childhood was full of joy and happiness.

My mother wrote a book named 'Utpala'. It was based on spirituality. The book is based on the glory of Seraikela's first deity,' Goddesses Paudi'. The simple language, the clear storyline had caught the attention of the readers. With the blessing of goddesses Paudi Seraikela has prospered in every field; all of them agree to this. To achieve success in every field, the people of Seraikela worship Devi Paudi irrespective of class, creed, and religion and also get the blessings of the goddesses. The world is based on faith and devotion to god. It stimulates each one therefore goddesses Paudi is always reverend.

There were certain rules and regulations which the royal family followed and adhered to it. But as the royal family stuck to the rules, regulations, and norms of the society to carry out the administration process so the general public tried to stay away from us though we were bonded together with the string of love and affection. Our family members could easily mingle with the general public. We involved ourselves in various cultural programs, festivals, and meetings and could get immense happiness.

The river Kharkai flows touching the palace. The river water is clear and transparent. The river flows amongst the beauty of nature and has helped in building a happy and prosperous life. On the bank of the river, there are many prosperous villages. In this river, girls take bath, play, and spend their time as if the river has bound them with love and affection. We play many games on its bank. We take bath in the river, play, and swim. Others also did the same on the other side of the bank of the river. All are equal for Maa Kharkei. During the month of Kartik, Kartik Snana, on Poornima, Poornima Snana, Makar Snana, Bahdujagaran, etc were performed during various festivals and auspicious days. Other than that we also participated in Asthapahari and Nama Jagya. Later on, these propitious activities had a deep impact on my life which everyone will agree with. Sometimes we arranged competitions like doll games and kaudi games for entertainment purpose. It was a fun time for us at that time.

Sareikela is famous for the Chhau dance. It still exists in the cultural heritage of Sareikela. My brothers, Subhendra, Brajendra, and Sudhendra had gained name and fame in Chhau dance. Subhendra gained name and fame abroad which was not only a proud moment for Sareikala but also for India for its rich cultural heritage. My brothers who were experts in Chhau dance visited Europe and other western countries along with their troupe and were appreciated. The scholars, artists, playwrights, writers, reporters, politicians, authorities, philanthropists, and others appreciated and praised the presentation of this art form.

My brother Subhendra Narayan once presented the Chhau dance in front of Mahatma Gandhi in Calcutta. At that time along with Gandhiji , there were Biswa Kobi Rabindranath Tagore, Sarojini Naidu, and the famous playwright Uday Shankar. They were fascinated by this dance form. At that time they experienced and appreciated the art form and said that amidst the darkness of subordination, the country's art, culture, and literature is like a lamp that evades darkness. The rigidity of British rule can't withstand the fundamental concept of Indian society. The art and culture of India didn't get shattered under the British monarchy rather it flourished with the encouragement of the royal family.

My father showed his interest in art, dance, music, and literature. My uncle Late Bijay Pratap Singh Deo took the pleasure of dance and music. My father wrote the play

'Shaibya' which was enacted many times under the direction of my uncle. Every time the audience enjoyed the play earnestly. The state of Sareikela is proud of that.

My elder brother Tikayat Nrupendra Narayan's book 'Sareikela and Kharsawan through the Ages' have a vivid description of Chhau dance. The book gives an insight into Chhau dance and the cultural heritage of Sareikela.

Every year 4 to 5 days before Pana Sankranti as per the decided day and time our festival begins and ends on Pana Sankranti. 13 Bhagats from different caste and creed assemble at the Shiva temple at a particular time. They take bath and wear the sacred thread and perform the rituals .Though they belonged to various castes and creed there was no differentiation between them. They thought of themselves as one family. They had their food only once in day at the Shiva temple. Among these 13 Bhagats there was one head Bhagat. He was known as the Pata Bhagat. They took bath at a particular ghat. That place was known as Marjana Ghat or the King's Ghat. In between, one day they perform Ghata Yatra. Many people come to see this. This traditional festival attracts many spectators. They get captivated by this with enthusiasm.

Pata Ghatua carries the ghata on his head and dances to the tune of music on his way to the Shiva temple. The Pata Ghatua wears a red colour dress and smears his body and face with vermilion. He wears different types of traditional jewelry and other Bhagats dress in traditional attire. This procession comes and stops near the ground in front of the palace. Chhau teams from Babu Sahi, Brahaman Sahi, Khatara Sahi, Kansari Sahi participate in this. They go and occupy their respective places to give their performance which was marked by a flag. Chhau dance is performed for 3to 4 nights.

could go without any difficulties from India evading the eyes of the Britishers. King Shankar Pratap had some knowledge regarding this because before he escaped, during the last moment of this incident he discussed with him to give him the car of Dhenkanal state bearing the state number and flag on a particular day at a particular time. Netaji said that the car will go up to the station and return but why the car will go and who will go in the car will not be asked by the owner of the car.

The arrangement began but what will happen on the final day wasn't known to King Shankar Pratap still he had some information regarding this. He never revealed it in front of anyone. Everything between them was inkling. During the preparation, Netaji Subhash Chandra Bose and King Shankar Pratap had a general conversation regarding the freedom struggle movement in the country. Netaji discussed with few reliable and trustworthy people at that time to keep himself away from any type of suspicion because the spy police of the British government had spread its tentacles to collect information regarding the future planning and activities of Netaji Subhash Chandra Bose.

The spies were unable to get any information regarding the activities. Because of this reason King Shankar Pratap was in the suspicious eyes of the spy police and the higher officials. They monitored all his activities very closely. As A Class king of a state, they couldn't take any immediate step or action against him. They always had an aim to prove him as a king who is a traitor to British rule, to punish him, and to arrest him. The family relationship between King Shankar Pratap and Netaji Subhash Chandra Bose was age-old. It began with the intimate liaison of Netaji's father Janaki Bose and King Shura Pratap. At that time Janaki Bose was a known lawyer and was also the guardian of King Shankar

The Chhau dance of Sareikela is incomparable. Chhau dance has been appreciated at the International level. There is a saying regarding Sarekela's Chhau dance.

Kharsuar ra jatra ghata, brahamania ghatiapata
Korara ra kalika ghata, Sarekela nata

I have heard that my grandfather, father, and uncle during their childhood use to perform Chhau dance with them. Those who performed Chhau dance in the family were appreciated and motivated in different ways. I have seen my brothers performing the Chhau dance. The special trait of Sarekela Chhau dance is the performer doesn't use a mask. My brother's expression on the face was very realistic and a spectator goes into trans seeing the performance. Mayurbhaj, Purulia, Dhenkanal, and Nilagiri also have mastered over the Chhau dance and they don't use a mask.

At present, there is no initiative taken from the government for the development of Chhau dance in Mayurbhanj and Purulia.It has lost its charm with time. Just for namesake it is performed in Dhenkanal .With the initiative of Maharaja Shura Pratap Mahendra Bahadur and his son Shankar Pratap Sigh Deo Balarampur, Kasiadihe, Jhuudia, Ganjaedehi(Chandra Sekhar Prasad) and in other villages there are 3 to 4 Chhau dance troupes which have achieved success. They made a provision to give some estate to the Chhau dance artists and Paika akhada. A renowned maestro of Mayurbhanj taught these troupes regularly.

Dhenkanal's Chhau dance troupe was awarded at Cuttack for their performance in a competition. In various cultural competitions, the Chhau dance troupe, Girls Guide, and Scouting gave their performance and brought laurels to Dhenkanal. But at present Chhau dance is on the verge of extinction. It just remains as a story from the past.

Dhenkanal's Chhau troupe had once gained name and fame. The cultural trend, generosity, and ideology prevailed at that time when compared to the present society and the government's callous attitude is slowly heading towards destruction.

The Chhau dance artists came from various backgrounds those who had an interest in it, those who were healthy, those who had good physic, and those who weren't suffering from any ailments. The most important thing which was considered to include these artists in the troupe was self-discipline. If a person was found disciplined and devoted towards the institution, irrespective of the caste and creed, poor or wealthy he was included in the troupe. The dance wasn't only confined to the royal family; it was rather of the country.

The royal court not only helped the Chhau dance artists but also helped those who were involved in cultural activities. The artists were encouraged by different means and modes. They were rewarded and supported financially according to their capabilities. As a result, the artists were putting their best effort to be the best. In the troupe there was no discrimination as all of them had the same food, took the training, and participated in the competitions. In a group performance there was no distinction. All were judged by the same yardstick irrespective of being a king or the subjects. They worked together as one in a disciplined way.

The vigor and vitality filled the life of the artist with happiness. They helped each other and reciprocated well. They belonged to a different religion, different caste, different status, had different personalities and mind-sets but they were inspired by the ethics of the group and were under one umbrella. They had respect and responsibility towards each other and were devoted to their group or institution. Though they were in the clutches of sub ordinance, they very well knew about the values of human life. This isn't an imaginary story but a truth. At that time Gandhiji's un-touchability movement or Harijan movement didn't begin. Racial discrimination and untouchability prevailed all over the country. Many superstitious beliefs prevailed in various parts of the country. In spite of these our Seraikela's royal family didn't go by the prevailing norms of un-touchability, superstitions, and racial discrimination. There was constant effort to keep these away from the social programs and to bring a change in society. No one can deny this as it's recorded in history and literature forever.

    I was born to this royal family which was advanced and progressive .Right from the beginning of my life, I have learned ethic, conduct, disciplined life, and courtesy. This has motivated me. I can never deny that I got married and came to Dhenkanal with all the virtues. Before my marriage, the relationship between Dhenkanal and Seraikela royal family was maternal house and aunt's house. Now it turned to father in laws and son in law's house. There was a great bond between the two families and they influenced each other in many ways.

Chapter-IV

DHENKANAL DURING MY MARRIAGE

Maharaja Shankar Pratap was born in the year 1904. His father died in the year 1918 when he was 14 years old. He was a boy and was studying at Dhenkanal. He was too young to realize the importance of worldly life. He wasn't matured enough to take the responsibility of the state and the royal throne. His mother was mourning and his five little brothers were in distress. In this situation of obscurity, at a young age, young King Shankar Pratap left everything in the hands of god and determined his duty. It was one of his firm decision and a strong and steady commitment. After that, he never looked back. For his benefit and for the benefit of all with the blessings of the goddesses Bhagabati he proceeded in the path of reality.

After the death of my reverend father in law Shura Pratap, as king Shankar Pratap was minor from the year 1918 till 1928 British government's representative carried out the administrative work(Court of Wards).At that time his guardian was Barrister Janaki Nath Bose, Shri Prafulla Sharkar, Rai Bahadur Shri Raj Kishore Tripathy, Kabiraj Shri Bala Krushna Nanda, Shri Basudev Pattanaik and the principal of Raj Kumar college Shri V.A.S Stow , Mr. Smith

Pears and Jadunath Sarkar. The administrative work, rules, and regulations which were followed in Dhenkanal were similar to the British rule in Mugalbandi areas.

If British rule is said to be progressive, advanced, and independent then like Mugalbandi areas, Dhenkanal from the year 1918 till 1925 was also progressive according to the yardstick.

At that time the British government ruled over the Mugalbandi areas ruthlessly. Exploitation was its height that's why mass movement or independence movement couldn't transpire in Mugalbandi areas. Such type of movement was ruthlessly sabotaged by the British government and its appointed agents. In that way, Dhenkanal was progressive to a certain extent. At that time the financial condition of India had degraded and the only reason for this was that the British government relentlessly collected revenue from the emperors, kings, landlords, and the people for their vested interest.

The revenue which was collected wasn't utilized for the benefit of the people. The British rulers never solved the problems that cropped up in Mugalbadi areas rather they ruled over the people barbarously. During natural calamities like flood and famine, the people of Mugalbadi areas died like a dog and suffered the loss. Though this happened in Mugalbandi areas regularly but no one could gather the courage to stand up against it.

The consequences of asking for help were dreadful but the kings and the landlords were always ready to render immediate help to the people of Mugalbadi areas. Dhenkanal's King Bhagiratha Mahendra Bahadur, Shura Pratap Mahendra Bahadur during the famine and in difficult times helped the people with food grain supply, education, and sanitation which is unforgettable and also a matter of pride. In the year 1935, during Boluchistan earthquake to help the people, the Dhenkanal court administration donated Rs 1000 which is equal to Rs 50,000 at present. Boluchistan is at present a part of Pakistan. Dhenkanal's royal family has never pulled its hand during any type of help. This praiseworthy work of Dhenkanal's royal family is appreciated by everyone. \

During World War I, grant was given to the Indian Army, Cuttack's Shri Rama Chandra Bhanja Medical College, Raipur's Rajkumar College, and Cuttack's Ravenshaw College's Kanika Library. For Vinoba Bhavae's Bhoodan movement 1000 acres of land was donated other than that various temples, institutes, and various volunteer organizations also received assistance. When I remember today about their work of charity, benevolence, and compassion I feel proud of them. The British rule appointed personnel in Mugalbandi areas had a fear of Gadjat kings and landlords.

The reason for the fear was, at any time they may report the activities of them to the British government and if needed may ask for judgment. Because of this fear sometimes those personnel did a little bit of work for the people but as a symbol of a bad ruler, the British government was known for its exploitation. As the princely state kings were benevolent, god-fearing, and had the urge for independence, later on, the Independence movement started but it couldn't begin in Mugalbadi areas due to the brutality of the British rulers. Many eminent persons of those areas started their struggle for freedom movement from the princely states.

In the year 1921, when Dhenkanal was under the Court of Wards the property tax was increased. There was a hike of 1 paisa. The increase in tax created unrest among the people. They requested not to bring a hike in the tax but as the Court of Ward was under the British government their request wasn't granted. The provocation of the leaders of Mugalbandi areas and the denial of rationalistic programs gave rise to an uproar in Dhenkanal at that time.

King Shankar Pratap never paid attention to petty issues because he was independent- minded and progressive. He raised his voice against British personnel's unnecessary interference and power display. He was able to justify himself as he was very knowledgeable. As he was an independent-minded person, he never accepted anyone's interference. He limited his disposition to his work ethic and never brought it to the knowledge of others. He hated self-propaganda. Due to this people adored him and he could make his place in the hearts of people. Regarding this, a true incident is narrated which reflects his love for the country, progressiveness, and knowledge.

I can't remember the year, month, or date but it was during the peak time of British rule. We were travelling from Cuttack to Calcutta and our luggage was carried to a specific compartment. At that time an Anglo-Indian man was sitting there carelessly and was reading a book. Raja Sahib and I were standing on the platform. The Anglo Indian man who was sitting there used abusive language and started shouting at the man who was carrying our luggage. He used slang in English.

The white man was very angry but we couldn't understand the reason. Raja Sahib pretended as if he neither saw nor heard anything and didn't react. He told me,' I think this person is sitting in the compartment without a ticket'. By that time the man who was carrying the luggage was in complete fear after the white man's berating. White men had a lot of power at that time. They detested the black-skinned people and they thought that there is no law for them. Raja Sahib asked the potter, 'What happened'? Why is he shouting like this? Do you understand regarding what is he scolding?

The man who was carrying our luggage said while keeping the luggage the corner part of the box touched his feet'.' Why are you so scared'? asked Raja Sahib. At that time the kings were given many facilities. According to that, the train won't move until Raja Sahib climbs the compartment and no one can occupy a seat in the compartment allotted to him without his consent. Raja Sahib was standing on the platform. It was already time for the train to leave but the guard could neither blow his whistle nor wave the flag for the departure of the train. How will the train move without taking the Dhenkanal's Raja Sahib?

The guard also didn't have the power to tell Raja Sahib to get on the train because it may seem like an order from the guard to Raja Sahib. At that time all were aware of their capacity. A little bit of deviance can lead to serious consequences. As the guard couldn't find out anyway so he came to Raja Sahib very cautiously and politely to say- Raja Sahib if you board the train then the train will move. Raja Sahib wanted this. He asked, how come you have allowed this great person to sit in our compartment? The guard was in a helpless condition. As the man sitting in the compartment was a white man so how could he tell him to go to another compartment? To ease the situation Raja Sahib told the white man, if you show the guard your ticket, he will make you sit in the right compartment.

As expected the white man started the fight and Raja Sahib said,' A person like you who is travelling without a ticket is undesirable or a person who is born in this land with the name of his forefathers is undesirable? A person like you who doesn't have any entity, how can that person be so abusive to a person who is born in this land? Is it justified'? The man was helpless at that time. He said, If he doesn't apologize to the potter then the king of Dhenkanal will not let the train move. The white man was bound to kneel and apologize to our man, the potter for his behavior. The train left the station. In the next station, Raja Sahib called the white man to our compartment and told him much realistic truths related to their future in the country. Whatever he professed will happen after independence became a reality. Along with the Britishers, many Anglo Indians also left India. Those who stayed back accepted the Indian nationality and lived as a citizen of India. These people don't have the pride at present which existed earlier and they are in penury.

A person who is continuing with his ancestral profession does have the self-respect, this mayn't be accepted by others but Dhenkanal's Raja Sahib Shankar Pratap during his reign never denied that. He can never appreciate a person who doesn't belong to this country showing his anger and rage on a person who is born in this country and belongs to this land. The white man filled with pride and ego apologized to a black man who was doing his family profession in the open platform is an example of racialism. Maybe many people might have ignored this incident and might have boarded the train but raja Sahib realized that it is an unpardonable act for the people of this country and himself so he said that the train won't leave the station unless the white man apologizes. Everyone knew that he had a good reputation during the British rule.

In the year 1925, at a very early age, he took over the responsibility of the reign and slowly entered into the state administration. From 1918 till 1925 when Dhenkanal was under Court of Wards and the administration wasn't fair he couldn't do anything regarding it. There was people unrest because of the hike in property tax. He discussed this issue with the knowledgeable people regarding its relevancy, utility, and patency.

The British government increased the property tax during Court Of Ward but it was less compared to other areas so people accepted it and didn't react much to it. All of them accepted the proposal calmly. Few self-centered people tried to be against the administration and instigated the people. Though King Shankar Pratap knew about the sedition but didn't pay much attention to it. If something is done for the benefit of the people then the result will be good, he believed in it. So he started working to enhance his skills as a good administrator and also brought changes in various sectors of administration. He aimed to rule the state conscientiously so that Dhenkanal prospers in every field. As he was a silent worker so no one could understand his ideology because of this a few self centered people took advantage and tried to spread the malignancy.

He slowly took up projects regarding how the forest will be protected, how the primary education will be made compulsory, how the students and parents will take initiative for higher education, how adult education will be initiated, how art, culture, and environment will be safe, how sports and scouting will be rewarded, how farmers and other skilled people will be successful, how people will be self-reliant and will lead a peaceful life. A lot of revenue was required to make these programs fruitful but at that time other than the property task and other regular tax there was no other source of income for the state.

These property tax and other taxes was also very less.

Whatever revenue was collected, out of that British government took its part and never gave any grant for the state development purpose rather pressurized the state and tried to collect revenue and many precious things from the state stating trivial reasons. Other than that there were also administrative expenditures. Despite of all these, there was development in Dhenkanal state. For every two or three villages one Primary School and one Secondary School were set up. People were involved in these types of programs as it was for the state. Teachers were also involved in this work.

There was good coordination between the teachers and the villagers and they worked in sync. The recognized village workers, the village teachers, and watchman regularly looked after the attendance of the students in the school, about its beautification, and also took care of its safety. The school management committee and Panchayat committee did various work and also monitored the school proceedings. At the time of need, the villagers did the work which the teacher and students couldn't think that it's their responsibility. The revenue needed to do the work was provided. The work which needed revenue to be accomplished was managed by the villagers. It was a combined effort.

King Shankar Pratap ministered to the protection of the forests and their natural resources. The people utilized the minimum resources from the forest like firewood, and other forest resources by paying a minimal forest tax. Other than that when people wanted to cut big trees for their personal use they followed the rule of planting three saplings and taking care of them for a year in return for cutting down a tree. People understood its necessity and benefits and accepted it and because of this the forest wasn't destroyed rather it expanded. The forest resources collected were kept carefully so that anyone could easily sustain them for three to four months.

Other than wood, Tendu leaves, berries, Mahula flower, Kanda roots and bulbs, honey, aromatic substances, bitter gourd, and leafy vegetables were collected from the forest. The king was a visionary and the forest protection program was a success. The villagers residing near the forest took care of the protection of the forest and the state administration encouraged them to do so. At that time science didn't flourish as per the present scenario still King Shankar Pratap because of his farsightedness could judge the things which were going to happen in the future. That's the reason why he worked for the protection of nature so that the animals and human beings can live a balanced life. He had to face the challenges and criticism of people but he never paid attention to it and judiciously went ahead with his work.

In the year 1937 or 1938, the rules and regulations which were applicable for the forests of Dhenkanal were appreciated in India. By the end of the court administration and with the beginning of the government of Independent India, Dhenkanal's forest resources were intact. If we would have intended, we could have sold the precious wood from the forest, it wouldn't have been against the rule but it was beyond our imaginations. These precious natural resources were under the state administration but King Shankar Pratap thought that it not only belongs to him but also belongs to the state and its people. He said though the forest resources were under Dhenkanal's jurisdiction but, its National wealth. He never allowed anyone to destroy it.

Many people are still alive at present who can genuinely speak regarding it. What happened to those forests? How and for what it got destroyed? In which work for the nation it could be utilized properly? If you search for the answers to these questions, will the Court administration will be pronounced as responsible? Those who worked aimlessly without putting their efforts, those who didn't realize the actual problem and kept themselves away from experiential education, those who misguided others ,they tried their best to destroy the resources.

The selfish political leaders and employees for their personal benefit didn't think about the benefit of the nation and cut down the trees from the forest without paying any price and destroyed the forest resources. The independence which we got from the sacrifice of people, these so called established and corrupted people misused it and utilized it for their personal benefits. Is it leadership? Is it nationality? Is it public service or service to the nation? At present the mountains and forests of Dhenkanal are barren. They have acquired the land illegally but couldn't be punished.

Underneath the mask of service to the nation, all the selfishness and sin committed by them are hidden. They projected their work in such a way that people appreciated them. After destroying the age old natural resources now these people in the name of the revival of the forest are utilizing the grant amount for their benefits and the barren lands are still barren. Maybe the people of this country are helpless but what about the people in this world? Can't they realize the truth? Today they accept the rules and forest protection acts of King Shankar Pratap which was prevalent at that time and they realize its necessity.

At present India is devoid of forests and turning into a desert and the farsightedness and service to the human race of King Shankar Pratap are highly accepted. But at that time few selfish people instigated the general public regarding this and created chaos. They tried to associate the politically influenced people of Odisha in this matter to create havoc. But those people realized that there is nothing wrong with this and kept quiet. In few places, the political leaders of other places tried to influence the general public to establish their leadership. Raja Sahib never felt disheartened by this.

He was also interested in the conservation of wild animals. If they grow in the natural habitat then there is no loss for anyone. Rather it's a gain. With the increase of wild animals in the forest the rate of destruction of the forest decreases because of fear. He made arrangements to capture the man eating tigers. When the number of elephants increased and they destroyed the crop at that time instead of killing them they were brought to be used for government affairs. The trap was laid to capture elephants and the help of people was taken for this work. Money was spent on this from the state treasury. But this wasn't enough .Some amount was misused without our knowledge. Few of them worked for capturing elephants at their own will and the few workers were paid for this work.

Sometimes because of the increase in the elephant population, elephants destroyed the crops and killed people so the elephant capturing program was helpful for people. But few selfish motive people took the advantage of this and tried to defame the state administration. But regarding the begar system whatever was told was the creation of few selfish people which projected their ill intention and self- centeredness. These people day and night worked against the state administration. Sometimes the hunting activity was also initiated.

At that time hunting was one of the royal sports but a few rules and regulations were followed. The general public was issued a license or permitted for such activities. During the animal birth season and in conserved forests hunting was prohibited. Overall the hunting game was carried out under rules and regulations and focused on displaying benevolence towards the animals and birds.

The British government never extended its helping hand for the development of the state in any regard. With the limited earning of the state, extreme care was taken for the development of the roads, water resources for irrigation, digging well for drinking water, etc. But as the developmental process was slow and wasn't getting completed in the stipulated time so the help of the public was sought.

The public also appreciated this keeping in mind the development of the state. Those who had the ill intention, destructive thoughts, and the nit pickers never appreciated it .Today we use the respectable term 'People's Participation 'for this. Which means 'For the people and By the people'. This was a derogatory term at that time which was known as 'Begar'. Today after 45 years of Independence still the Begar system and donation of labor exist even though a lot of money is invested for any construction work. The construction work for which so much of money is invested, it is doubtful if it can be ever get completed or if it's completed then the structure will sustain or after few years it will collapse. It happens that the basic plan changes at the time of construction. In the case of digging a well, before the water stream sprouts from the well, the well is filled with water and it is said that the well has plenty of water, a false report is made and the amount is disbursed.

Most often the construction of well, road, and bridge only exist on the paper while in reality it never exists. Still, no one responds. For all the construction work a large amount of money is sanctioned, a little is used for this purpose, and the rest is distributed among a few people. Because of this the problems faced by people is increasing day by day. There is no availability of water for drinking purpose or irrigation, there is no canal, if it exists then it's half constructed, there are no rooms in the school, if exist then either it's half constructed or in a dilapidated condition.

There are no teachers, if teachers are there then there is no facility for them to give proper education. There is no standard of education. Students use unfair means in the examination. In the name of development in the industry sector a lot of money is invested whereas the farmers are neglected. The farmers are the worst sufferers and their financial condition is deteriorating day by day. Neither encouragement nor any help is provided to them. They struggle in their life to maintain their family. 80 % of the population of the country depends on agriculture but their pain and plight remain unheard and unseen. But at that time it wasn't so. All of them worked and gave their best according to their abilities. There was no question of duping. In the villages, people worked together according to their skills.

In every field of work, the employees of the king involved themselves to look after it. They visited the villages, took care of the schools, student's attendance, teacher's work, games, scouting, farming, health, and forest protection. The higher officials of the king's administration were imparted with training to enhance their skills and knowledge so that they can take care of any department if assigned. King Shankar Pratap himself encouraged them. He properly guided them to be the best in their field of activity. After the princely states joined Dhenkanal, many old employees of Dhenkanal's King's administration according to their skills and knowledge were appointed in the Odisha government as higher officials. They could display their skills, abilities, thoughts, and ideology in their work field as they were well trained by the Dhenkanal's king's administration. This is accepted and realized by everyone.

He appointed the knowledgeable and dedicated people as the principal of the High school and as government teachers so that the standard of education is enhanced and values are inculcating among the students. Similarly intelligent and brilliant individuals were appointed in various departments for smooth and better functioning. Among them were the higher officials who retired from the British government like- Devan Bahadur Dayanidhi Das, Devan Rai BahadurBraja Bihari Burman, Commissioner of Police Rai Bahadur K.B Rai, Dist. Addl. Session Judge Rai Bahadur Bhabdeb Sarkar, Chief Minister Mandhata Gorachand Pattanaik, was a renowned lawyer at Berhampur and a member of Madras Law Council, and also a minister during British rule in Paralakhemundi Maharaja's ministry. By the time the administration took over the developmental work with these suitable and educated personnel, 6 to 7 years had passed. Throughout India, people were driven by political consciousness and to get independence the kings and the people of the state worked together.

There is another face of life in Indian tradition where the married couple seeks a child. At that time we didn't have any children so my mother- in- law and grandmother-in -law were worried. There were very pious and performed many sacred ceremonies so that we will be blessed with a child. Sometimes we entrusted the administration work to the hands of experienced employees and went for pilgrimage and visited many scenic places. The primary reason for visiting these places was to perform the sacred rituals to attain peace, to realize the importance of scenic beauty, to know about the administrative procedure of other states, and the lifestyle of their subjects.

During our visit to the pilgrimage, we performed the rituals for the benefit of people and the state. We worshipped, did the charity to get the blessings so that the ritual performed will be fruitful. Those were the religious rituals that were mostly performed at that time. It was not controversial. This tradition still exists and nothing has changed. We got immense peace of mind and satisfaction while performing these rituals. As we didn't have children so we also went through pain and agony in our life but we didn't give up. There was sadness but we didn't break down in lamentation. We both were god fearing, always realized the presence of divine power, and thought that at one point of time we will be blessed by the god. Though not directly but in an indirect way we were always blessed by God.

King Shankar Pratap mingled with the local people without any hesitation wherever we stayed during our visit to different places. He never felt proud of himself as the king of a state. He never tried to reveal his true identity in front of them. He was known as Shankar among them but because of his gifted personality and the polished language, he captivated them. At many times he discussed philosophy and mythology with many knowledgeable people and illustrated his deep knowledge. People were enticed by his deep knowledge. He was known among the local people in unknown places irrespective of rich, poor, literate, and illiterate as an adorable personality.

He was conferred with Vidyasagar title when he was

in Kasi which is known academically and religiously for his knowledge. It was a highly respected title at that time and was decided by the learned scholars of Kashi after thorough scrutiny. Few envious people tried to disgrace him but couldn't raise their voice in front of the learned scholars. His personal life was excellent and ideal and as he was popular so many envious people tried to harm him .King Shankar Partap was fortuitous and courageous; the dirty remark of these people couldn't alter his personality. He neither gave up nor bowed his head down in front of these envious, empty headed people. He was calm, composed, and poised. He was victorious and an epitome of humanity.

He was independent by his thoughts. He hated the British rulers and the British government and also didn't trust them. The reason was, the British government looked down upon the heritage and religion of the country and tried to create indifference among the people, and treated them cruelly. As he was the ruler of the state so he couldn't resist this directly but at many times as a silent protestor, he didn't cooperate with them. Sometimes he disapproved of their unfair, unjust, and written instructions or very firmly brought it to the knowledge of the ruling authority.

During his reign, he disdained the British government because of his knowledge and intelligence. As a result, the employees of the British government were afraid of him and were very active in finding faults with him but, were unable to do so. At that time to disobey and to confront the most powerful British government wasn't a small thing. King Shankar Pratap was under the suspicious eyes of the British government. They were waiting for a chance to convict him. In this situation, King Shankar Pratap was able to save himself because of his patience and courage.

To know, to be known, and to make others realize his value, he met the learned and knowledgeable people like renowned writers, reporters, judiciary, patriots, and locally prominent people and recounted his matter of contemplation. He met and discussed with Mahatma Gandhi, .Jawaharlal Nehru, Sardar Vallabhbhai Patel, Chakravarty Rajgopalchari, Netaji Subhash Chandra Bose, Asif Ali, Aruna Asaf Ali , Muhammad Ali Jinnah, Prafulla Sarkar, Biju Pattanaik, Sir Tej Bahadur Sapru, Doctor Bidhan Chandra Ray, Doctor H.C Mukherjee, Sir M.C Setalvad, Godabarish Mishra, Nilakantha Das, Nalin Ranjan Sarkar, Sarojini Naidu, Prafulla Chandra Sen, Sir Robinson, V.P Menon, Shri P.C Sarkar, B hupesh Gupta, Dhiren Dey, Biswanath Dash, Doctor S. Radhakrishnan, Doctor Rajendra Prasad, Lal Bahadur Sastry, M.C Chigla, M.K Dey,Justice Ranganath Mishra, Shri Lokanath Mishra, Krishna Menon, Sardar Panikar, Dr. Harekrushna Mahatab Dr. Radhanath Rath, Shri Neelamani Routray, Shri Neren Ghosh, Shri Harihar Dash, Shri Lokanath Chowdhary,His Excellency Sir H.C Mukherjee,Dr.Jakir Hussain, Shri Lokanath Mishra,Dr.Kalidash Nag,Smt.Padmaja Naidu,Shri Sadik Ali,Smt. Violet Alva, Rai bahadur Raghbendra Banerjee,I.P Barristar,Sir J.C Mukherjee,Sir V.P Singhrai, Sir Biren Mukherjee,General Sikandar Mirja,Gopal Swarup Pathak, Sir Birakishore Rai, Chief justice and other eminent personalities.

It was a matter of appreciation. Despite of the difficult situations and circumstances, he met them without the knowledge of the British administration. It was one of the steps taken by a brave and revolutionary person like him. He kept this to himself and never did propaganda about himself, as a result, a handful of self centered people tried to project him as a controversial personality. But King

Shankar Pratap detested that as he was righteous. This isn't a preconceived story, it's the utter truth.

Sardar Valabh Bhai Patel had respect for King Shankar Pratap and also he was very friendly with him. He trusted him a lot. The king also had an amicable relationship with Jawaharlal Nehru. He met Mahatma Gandhi many times to discuss regarding the Swaraj Movement. He discussed with him the plans of the movement and how to initiate it further. Mahatma Gandhi wasn't only happy with the discussion with King Shankar Pratap but also confided in him. These things didn't come to light as he never did the publicity.

Gandhiji considered King Shankar Pratap as an important person because of his independent perception as a Gadajat king. To unravel the reality of the aforesaid I would like to narrate a story. Still, many people who are alive those who know this incident personally. They can throw light on this. A human being for his personal gains tries to hide the truth, covers up the false, and makes stories. He tries to build a castle in the air to impress others. It was in the year 1942. A telegram was sent to Mahatma Gandhi from Dhenkanal. It was sent by a man who was educated and had technical knowledge. It was written" The king of Dhenkanal is torturing the people of Dhenkanal, killing them ruthlessly and after that throwing their dead bodies in the river Bramhani. People are fleeing to save their life. Please intervene in this matter and save the lives of people.'

Earlier, Mahatma Gandhi had discussions with King Shankar Pratap and he knew about his temperament so he didn't believe in what was written in the telegram. He could easily understand the motive of pretentious people and had sent a social worker who was very courageous to find out about the authenticity of the situation at Dhenkanal. He came and mingled with people discussed with them. He met the leaders and discussed with them. He also discussed with the court administration and Raja Sahib frankly. After he was convinced about the reality of the situation, he sent a telegram to Mahatma Gandhi and informed him that it was a completely false allegation with a vested interest which is baseless.

All over India, there was a public awakening to be free from British rule, so was in Dhenkanal. It can be said that this movement was against British rule rather than against King Shankar Pratap. Shri Sarangdhar Dash received a scholarship from King Shura Pratap's court and went to Japan to pursue his study in Sugar Technology. But he left Japan without permission and went to America so the court of the king excluded him from the scholarship. Later on, he returned from America and gave a proposal to open a sugar factory at Dhenkanal and seek help.

King Shankar Pratap took the initiative and helped him and other than that he made arrangements so that Shri Sarangdhar can take money as a loan from his mother and grandfather. In the Kamakhya Nagar subdivision in Odisha, the village now known as Damsal , the sugar factory was established. The fields were fertile so there was a good harvest of sugarcane crop. He was allowed to sell the wood and other natural resources which were found in abundance in that land. The revenue generated from this was allowed to be used in the sugar factory. If the sugar factory comes up then people of Dhenkanal will get a job, sugar will be used all over the country, the farmers will use the modern technology for sugarcane cultivation, they will earn money and Dhenkanal will be praised. Keeping this in mind King Shanakar Pratap immediately worked on it. But it didn't work out and all his efforts went in vain.

Few people try to cover up the truth cunningly, bring into light the fallacy to create a fictitious history. Society blindly follows the historians and continues with the distorted history. As a result, the distorted history is accepted in society and the future generation follows it. Netaji Subhas Chandra Bose left the country to make India independent is an astonishing episode.

Subhas Chandra Bose's disappearance and Baji Rout's death are such astonishing events. In the year 1941, in the month of January, we went to Calcutta. As I was expecting, so for my medical check-up I ,Raja Sahib, my brother in law Shri Gourendra Pratap Singh Deo with the state car were staying in a rented house in Dhenkanal Staff Calcutta 6, Elgin Road. At that time Subhash Chandra Bose was under a house warrant and was staying in his family house in Elgin Road. King Shankar Pratap sometimes went to his house to meet him. As he was a ruler of A Class state so he had many privileges and when he travelled by his car bearing a red number plate and a flag of Dhenkanal state spy police didn't create any problem for him.

As per my knowledge, just 2 to 3 days before Netaji disappeared; King Shankar Pratap went to meet him. I have heard that the driver of Dhenkanal state car no 5 who was a resident of Dhenkanal town, Late Shri Kanhu Charan Singh along with a staff Shri Balabhadra Parida carried a letter from King Shankar Pratap to Netaji. I have also heard that Dhenkanal state car bearing the red number plate and the flag helped Netaji in his disappearance; but twelve years old boy says that he drove the car under strict patrolling, without a license and helped Netaji to disappear.

Many days after the incident, many of them dug the history and beaconed that, it's because of the courageous steps taken by few people Netaji Subhash Chandra Bose

Pratap after the death of his father King Shura Pratap. There were good rapport and intimacy between them. Both the families were closely associated with each other.

Later on, as King Shankar Pratap was in need, he purchased the house and the land which was in 14 Camac Street and belonged to the family of Janaki Bose. Today also that house and land exist. Right from childhood King Shankar Pratap and Netaji Subhash Chandra Bose draw nearer because of the family association and also because they shared the same ideology. As per the invitation of Netaji Subhash Chandra Bose for the Calcutta Congress session, he along with his relatives sat in the audience gallery and watched the program right from the beginning till the end.

At that time Congress was actively taking initiative to initiate the freedom for struggle movement against British rule and it wasn't a small matter for a king of a state to join the Congress session. King Shankar Pratap's reflection regarding independence is admirable. He could slightly project himself in limelight and reflected his own thoughts and program of action in a very subtle way. King Shankar Pratap was genial, triumphant and was known for his incomparable personality. He never tried to bring himself to the limelight so he faced unnecessary inconvenience but he didn't lose his true identity. He never accepted others' authoritativeness and never accepted defeat.

According to Netaji's instruction on a particular day and at a particular time the state car bearing the red number plate and flag reached the place. The driver was Late Kanhu Charan Singh He feels proud when he narrates that he could leave Netaji Subhash Chandra Bose safely at his destination in our car. Many of them feel surprised and happy when they listen to this incident from him. As it was the Dhenkanal king's vehicle so the spy police officials and the railway employees though suspected but couldn't dare to inspect the vehicle. As a result, Netaji Subhash Chandra Bose according to his plans could escape without the British administration's knowledge.

After reaching outside India when Netaji declared that India should get independence and the Britishers should leave India immediately, at that time the British administration was baffled. They tried their best to capture Netaji Subhash Chandra Bose and to take action against those people who had helped Netaji to flee. King Shankar Pratap experienced immense satisfaction and was elated as he could contribute a little in his little way to help Netaji to realize his dream of independent India. But he never proclaimed it nor gave a chance to anyone to throw light on it. The way he had helped the true patriot Netaji Subhash Chandra Bose in his own way is an example of the thought process of an independent personality. This can't be denied.

The British government tried its best to bring charges against him as an offender because of many reasons. He had a lot of faith in his religion, work, culture, and heritage, had love and affection for his subjects, was generous in his administration, had love a for his country, and nation and not last but the least his abhorrence for the British ruler and its employees certainly was a reason for being in the suspicious eyes of the British administration. There was no doubt about it. British administration left no stone unturned to find out the fault in him and to convict him. As Dhenkanal was A Class state so according to the rules they couldn't interfere directly or charge him openly.

Due to our pilgrimage, holy rituals, and worship finally we were blessed with a child after 17 years of marriage. The rituals, worship and donations didn't go in vain. Our religion saved us but for that, we went through physical and mental distress. After 17 years of marriage on 06.08.1941 on the auspicious full moon day of the Hindu month of Shravana (Shravan Poornima),after performing the rituals of Devi Kamakshi and Ramchandi with the blessings of the goddesses our son Kamakhya Prasad was born.

King Shankar Pratap had devoted his time in state administration for 3-4 years before our marriage. He appointed the trained and skilled people in his administration. These people underwent rigorous training to improve their mental ability and self confidence so that they take appropriate decisions according to the situation. When we went for the pilgrimage few of them were influenced by the atrocious entities and got themselves involved in heinous activities in our absence. To make a fortune they initiated Begar system and collected revenue. The impact of this was on the king or the head of the administration.

Usually when a yogi, a beggar, a guest or a kinsman comes to the village, the villagers treat them properly. It was a tradition of Dhenkanal. But the humanity and magnanimous activity turned into oppression by few self centered people. The effect of this was not only on people but also on us which was unexpected. Few things like this occurred without our knowledge. We were completely kept in dark. The report which reached us was well written by these solipsistic and all of them said that everything is going on well.

The kind hearted and simple King Shankar Pratap believed what was told to him and was unable to figure out the mistakes. Any married couple, whether the king or the subject is in sorrow until they are blessed with a child. They feel disheartened. Life becomes an inferno. We also faced this in our life. Thought of those days bewilders me.

At that time we were disheartened and had an aversion towards life and we decided that we will renounce everything and go to a deserted area in the foothills of the Himalaya and spend our lives in an ashram.

King Shankar Pratap made a note on this and it is mentioned in Annexure. His inner conscience is reflected in this. Because of the personal dilemma, he made up his mind to pull out from the worldly pleasures and the state administration. He wasn't fascinated by the royal cornucopia or the parochial. He envisaged an ambrosial world. The internal situation was dismal and there was dissatisfaction in the administration. When Kamakhya Prasad was born in the year 1941, the king was extremely happy and he decided to take a firm step to confront all odds.

He took stringent action against the people who initiated the Begar system and collected revenue from the people in the name of the king in his absence. He sacked a few corrupted people from their work. Those who tried to play tricks with his faith were debarred from the state administration. He took all the decision himself without depending on others in any matter and worked for the benefit of the people and Dhenkanal state.

By that time the Independence movement in India had already gained its momentum. 60 crore people of India followed the path of truth and nonviolence, confronted the British administration boldly. The British administration aimed to create indifference among the kings, caste, creed, and religion to continue its reign. Unlike the people of the country following the footsteps of non- violence to get independence.

King Shankar Pratap was against British rule right

from the beginning. The righteous and knowledgeable King Shankar Pratap had understood the true meaning of independence, dreamed of independence passionately, and followed the passion with truthfulness, bravery, and confidence. For King Shankar Pratap the independence movement had much value directly or indirectly that can only be assessed from the situation and the history. But he never wanted to be in the limelight so his contribution remained unseen and unheard. But what he never thought, never did, or never said was brought into the limelight by the atrocious people in an exaggerated way.

The British administration collected information from various sources and came to the conclusion that King Shankar Pratap was instrumental in Netaji Subhash Chandra Bose's escape and also associated with India's Independence movement, therefore punishable. With this allegation, the British administration took away the administrative power from King Shankar Pratap and entrusted in the hands of three officials of the British government which formed a committee to carry out the administration procedure.

The aim and purpose were to anyhow bring out allegations and charges against the king. The officials in the committee were Mr. Srivastav, T. Satyanarayan, and Shri Trivedi. They gave jobs, gave money, conferred people with honors, and also threatened imprisonment and told them to provide proof and become a witness against the king Other than that they collected a lot of money taking advantage of the situation. Those who were serving the king of Dhenkanal to get more and more money became false witnesses and gave their statement against the king. They even got jobs my speaking against the king.

Few of them projected themselves as the leaders of

the state. They did the propaganda that Dhenkanal's King Shankar Partap has lost all his wealth and power as he was against the British administration. But they could never realize that his patriotism. The background of the allegations that the British administration brought against the king was his patriotism and the Independence movement. Other than that these three people who were appointed showcased their power and created chaos. Their coercive acts were appreciated by the hoggish group of people. They had apathy towards the general interest.

King Shankar Pratap was never egoistic. He was a silent and brave revolutionary. He didn't tolerate the one sided administration and tyranny of the British government. He retaliated against it in front of the high commissioner bravely with proper justification to get proper justice. Before the judgment, there was an unknown fear which engulfed Dhenkanal.

They tried to frame charges against King Shankar Pratap but weren't able to succeed. If the charges weren't brought against the king then the British administration will be discredited so by hook or crook the char sheet should be prepared against the king. Though these three officials belonged to the country by birth and by religion but favoured British administration as they were appointed by them. They can never be the traitors. That's why they tried to create the fake situations and instigated fake people to give their statements against the king. They lost their conscience and didn't follow the law. They terrorized the people.

An important official of state administration and the king's third brother Nini Sahib was told to frame false charges against the king and to condemn his actions. As the allegation to be manifested was impractical, baseless, and false so Nini Sahib refused it at full throttle and he was imprisoned ruthlessly by the British administration. Similarly an official Nandakishore of the king's state administration who was working in the year 1940, resigned and retired from his work as he was forced to design false stories against the king. As he refused to do so, he was imprisoned and treated mercilessly.

Those who didn't raise their voice against the British administration, they were benefitted and were rewarded. They followed the direction of the British administration agents and became ruthless. Those who raised their voice against the British government were treated heinously. They sustained the barbaric act, didn't bow down in front of injustice, and went ahead with the independence movement which is a mark of their patriotism.

The king's other brother Tiki Sahib was performing a ritual of Maa Bagalmukhi for Graha shanti near Jaunli Pokhari Matha. The charges were brought against him that he is performing the tantra rituals to decimate British administration and its employees. To prove this they could even arrange witnesses in exchange for money. But, before he could be arrested he left Dhenkanal stealthily and went to Kashmir. Attempts were made to imprison him and to give him severe punishment but they couldn't succeed.

They were preparing one after another allegation against the king secretly. What information they were collecting wasn't known. We could understand that we are going to face an adverse situation very soon. There was also an allegation against me that I am selling kerosene and earning money in lakhs. I heard this on my way to Patna from Dhenkanal through Boudh. Nothing was impossible in the case of the British administration and their ignoble, hallow slaves at that adverse situation. I was terrified and filled with hatred when I came to know about the fabricated kerosene business of mine as if I didn't have any other work! I did a kerosene business?

How this false allegation did come into being? What didn't I have? I had the state, the reign, the authority, and property. More than all this- I had my family reputation, family tradition, dignity, and intelligence. How will my dignity enhance by this kerosene business was outside my understanding. I was unable to do anything and was shattered. We belonged to the Dhenkanal's royal family but we were tortured, we were suspected by the narrow-minded, selfish people, we were belittled that was only because of our disapproval and disdain of British administration and its officials. There was no doubt about it. We tried to encourage patriotism, the spirit, our culture, and heritage but it wasn't recognized at that time nor in the future rather was injustice done with us. Those who named us as traitors, their statements are unpardonable. Though we suffered and were punished but later on after independence we received the freedom fighter allowances and many facilities. We still get these facilities.

Many so- called leaders of that time though were disrepute presented their appreciation letter. They also received the benefits. This is what is patriotism, sacrifice, and benevolence. If we try to analyse this at present the truth becomes very clear. But no one took initiative at that time to bring the truth to the light. Though the truth has come into light but no one reacted to it because they could tactfully change the mind of the people. Afterward my brother the king of Balangir Late Rajendra Narayan Singh Deo came to know that my kerosene business was a fake and created issue, he presented this in front of the administration in a very polite but stern manner, he also mentioned the activities of the Dhenkanal agents condemned it and asked for immediate action. The charges on me regarding the kerosene business were lifted.

Poverty makes people weak. Leaving aside the wealthy and progressive families, the general public was devoid of basic education. Through the British agent, the reign of terror which was created in Dhenkanal and along with that the way the royal family was defamed, had an impact on King Shankar Pratap and he immediately asked for justice by writing a letter to the British administration. Other than that he met the higher official and Viceroy and discussed with them and wanted them to take immediate action. Though he was very calm and quiet by nature but he took this issue seriously and confronted the British administration.

He deciphered the rules and regulations, kept his self-esteem intact, and was able to come out of the Machiavellian policy of the British administration, and finally took over his reign. The British administration was defeated by King Shankar Pratap. The three British agents apologized for their mistake in fright. They were condemned for their atrocity and they thought King Shankar Pratap will act similarly so they thought of leaving the place at the earliest. But the king wasn't vindictive because they worked according to the instruction of the British administration and tried to be in their good books by stooping to such atrocities. There were devoid of inner conscience as they were born into slavery. They were detested by all.

It is necessary to discuss uprightly regarding the incidents that occurred in the year 1942 and before to bring into the light the reality of the incident which was grotesque for the sake of enlightening the truth. The kings in the country had the authority to reign over their states but the

British government came up with a law called 'Suryasta Law' under Clause- 6 the kings can be brought under British administration and work for them at any time and any place. In the name of peace if they entered any state with their British army then their authority will be considered.

The kings didn't have any power during that time in the state. According to the agreement other than the regular administrative work, the other things like political events and law and order were in their hands. The kings were very vigilant regarding the activities of the British officials. The freedom movement had already spread its wings and was taking up fiercely by that time. The British rule tried its best to suppress it. Their act to quash couldn't materialize in few states as they were directly ruled by the king.

The more they tried to squelch, the more the people became aggressive. Therefore the British administration tried to focus on a few states to snuff out to materialize their objective. As they had contacts with the Dhenkanal king's officials and as the general public had started the revolution against the British government so the responsibility of the Dhenkanal state was entrusted in the hands of resident and political agents according to the British administration to suppress the mass movement.

The king's court never requested this on its own. As the resident and political agents started their repressive operations the people who were directly related to the mass movement came and discussed with King Shankar Pratap in the king's court and gave the information regarding the mass movement. Shri Harmohan Pattanaik was a close friend of King's younger brothers, Tiki Sahib and Sana Sahib, and was also the classmate of Tiki Sahib. They were planning to start a business in Calcutta and Dhenkanal together. Their friendship was inseparable. Shri Baishnab Charan Pattanaik's brother of Late Bhakta Charan Pattanaik was working for the court administration.

As Baishnab Charana was involved in the mass movement so his brother wanted to leave the job as he apprehended that he may develop mistrust regarding the administration or some not so amenable situation may arise. Raja Sahib explained Bhakta babu calmly regarding this and permitted him to leave. Whether it was an example of benevolence or not, before that could be understood Bhakta babu himself felt obliged and was influenced by this great personality. King Shankar Pratap very adorably told him- Baishnab babu is using his intelligence and conscience and doing his work in his way and you will do your work in your own way using your intelligence and conscience. You are working hard to make your family sustain that is your duty. There is nothing to worry about it.

Nini Sahib, Tiki Sahib, Sana Sahib along with the poet and Communist leader Ananta Pattanaik and the revolutionary Rama Chandra Ram made three films named Lalita, Rolls 28, and Saptasajya. They could have never been able to do this unless they had social and cultural consciousness and had no social discrimination.

The police force which was under the resident and political agents came to Gadjat intending to continue its reign but it was very clear by that time that the British rule was coming to an end. So the British officials started their barbaric act of repression as per the instructions. King Shankar Pratap was feeling restless and helpless. He took an oath to help people in his own way. Where ever the British soldiers went for a road march or to supervise the villages, Raja Sahib informed that area beforehand and gave in writing to the British soldiers not to go there. He gave the instructions to the people to be careful and to keep the womenfolk and children in a safe place.

In that situation, the respect of the family shouldn't become a victim of the narrative that the family is a foreign agent or has ulterior motives. In this way, he protected many respectful and modest families from being disrespected. This is acknowledgeable. He immediately announced that those who will write an agreement letter that they are loyal to the court administration will escape from the vengeance of British soldiers. This was done with a motive to protect people from the torture because of this many people were saved and so was their family respect.

When the British soldiers prepared the list of people to be captured and the list of villages for flag march it was told to them that the people aren't revolutionaries and they don't intend to do any harm to them. Usually, they listened to the king and didn't pick up the people, if picked up they were left free and they didn't go to the villages for flag march. In this way many were saved. This noble act of King Shankar Pratap was also criticized at that time but, he didn't bother about this. Rather he was self-contented and helped the ignorant people directly or indirectly as he thought it was his prime duty.

It is a truth that the king and the administration are always blamed for any mistake. At that time the place Madhi in the year 1942 on the first birthday of my eldest Kamakhya Prasad was named Kamakhya Nagar. The court and the police station were burned, the royal employees were beaten and terror was created among them. In self defense, before they could get any orders it wasn't possible to take any action on humanitarian ground. Burning the property and beating the people was against the law. Those who did that were condemned and this isn't acceptable at present also. On the same ground in the year 1938 to oppress the Mass Agitation, the British government brought the police from other states like Punjab and clubbed with Kharswan, Seraikela, Khairagad, and Dhenkanal's police and formed Eastern State Agency Joint Police .

The people were carried away by the talks of Praja Mandali , they didn't listen, they became undisciplined finally to scare them firing was ordered. Gadjat police weren't given arms and ammunition. To chase away the protestors when the police fired Baji Rout died. Taking the death of Baji Rout in to account the rumors were spread that King Shankar Partap himself like Punjab's Jallianwala Bagh massacre had created another massacre in Nilakanthapur Ghat and had killed many people.

The death of Baji Rout had tormented King Shankar Pratap and we knew about it. He ordered the officials to justify the reason and situation for which such a thing happened and also ordered them to take action against it. They said that according to the law and the rules of the administration they were bound to do this as a part of their duty so no action could be taken against them. After the independence those who were a part of this agitation, among them few applied to receive the freedom fighter allowances, few of them received it and few were recruited as the higher officials in independent India administrative service where they have earned a lot of name and fame. Similar situations and circumstances have aroused at many times in independent India during the reign of the elected government directly or indirectly.

As a citizen of an independent country I feel, is it pride to silently accept that , to be scared and give silent support as the citizens of Republic India? Could anyone bravely oppose the independent Indian government and break it?

Could they deny that? The two innocent, calm, composed and hardworking boys Sunil and Bengapania protested and lost their lives as they were fired by the so- called elected government for a dispute regarding the demarcation of Odisha state border which was a case of injustice for the state. Did it agonize anyone? If they would have realized, they would have mourned for a few days but could anyone blame anyone for this?

Neither a commission was formed nor was an investigation report prepared. There was no memorial constructed in their names and their names aren't mentioned anywhere the history. Many people die of hunger, disease, and pain. There is neither enough money for treatment nor water for drinking though there are lakhs of wells, ponds, and tube wells. It seems the country is surviving based on hollow chemistry. At present, the influence of the powerful people is more and they think of their vested interest. As a result, the progress of the country has slowed down and innumerable people are left to suffer endlessly. They can't liberate themselves from this. Life is paralyzed.

After the end of the three agents' administration, the king began his reign with peace, law, and order. To run the work of each department swiftly the officials were instructed to function properly keeping the law and order in mind irrespective of caste creed, and religion. The king encouraged them to work fairly. Panchayat was created taking the elected members from the village. Under the Panchayat activity were the internal law and order, advanced farming facility, education and the functioning of educational institutions, protection of forest resources, Pucca house, and the increase in the basic resources and many more developmental facilities. Other than that a higher official committee was also appointed to give an unbiased and fair justice.

At that time this system and arrangement were appreciated by people. Many Gadjat states and officials from other states came to Dhenkanal to gain knowledge about this system and to implement it in their state. King Shankar Pratap discussed with them regarding this system and also regarding the pace of the independence movement. As a result, all of them were benefited and there was a change in their thought and work process and it took a new dimension. He tried to bring a change in his state, socially, culturally, and financially in the unfavourable condition of that time.

At that time there was a rapid change in the political scenario. The freedom movement was at its peak and the British government finally decided that they will finally declare India as independent and go back to England but will leave the venom of diplomacy. It happened. They divided the country into two parts according to language, caste, and religion and finally left. In the year 1947, August 15, India got its freedom and formed its government. There was a lot of happiness and excitement everywhere.

King Shankar Pratap was progressive and was proud of his language, culture, literature, and history. He raised his voice against superstitious beliefs, and action. He thought that superstitious belief is a hindrance in the path of progress. He always thought of the making of polished and cultured society. In the year 1935, a poor boy Shri Dharmendra Nayak came to the king to seek help for his higher education. He met the boy and was influenced by his simplicity and helped him. In the beginning, arrangements were made to keep him in the Jauli Pokahari Matha hostel. It wasn't a small matter at that time.

There was a protest against it but he gave a justified argument and made everyone silent. The stringent casteism couldn't overpower and force King Shankar Pratap to change his decision. The calm and quite brilliant student stayed in the hostel and completed his studies. Afterward he did a job and led a happy life. He understood that untouchability is a blot on society. To eradicate the caste system he took bold steps.

At that time in Dhenkanal, a specific community wasn't accepted by anyone. No one even drank water from their hand and they were segregated from society. This community faced a lot of problem, had an ill fate, and wasn't accepted by the society. This hurt King Shankar Pratap. He brought an amendment in this and gave this specific community a place in society. He discussed this with the scholars of Dhenkanal and Talcher and to give reorganization to this community he had sent Pundit Sekhareswara Mishra as a representative to Puri Muktimandapa's pundits to collect instruction based on the scriptures. Before taking this decision he discussed with me and others very clearly about casteism. In our Sareikela's royal family never any firm decision was taken against any community or family or about the caste system and because of that any family or people belonging to any caste were free to move around.

We discussed and concluded that it's not required to address anyone as untouchable. Our ideology helped him to take wise decisions. Anyway he never took a one-sided decision regarding any matter at any time and took everyone's advice. He took the advice of other honourable men, discussed the advantages and disadvantages and finally took his decision which is for the benefit of all. That is not only respectful but also an excellent principle. Not only this, but also sometimes he performed the marriage ceremony of the orphan girls according to their lineage and caste with dignity. He also helped in performing the sacred thread ceremony of the Braham children.

Irrespective of caste, creed, and religion he helped people and it was one of King Shankar Pratap's regular work. He did his work selflessly as he believed in the almighty God but a few narrow minded, selfish, and dissatisfied people criticized his act. If the poor, helpless, unhappy people wouldn't have come to the notice of such an affectionate king then their land, house, and property would have been enjoyed by the group of people who plot schemes, don't put any effort ,hard work, and don't invest money. The King's interference was a hindrance to this. That's why they kept themselves behind and spread the word that it's not a righteous work done by the king. Though we came to know about it we ignored it thinking that it's the work of the wicked people. How can a jealous and selfish person speak well?

To give justice impartially was only possible for King Shankar Pratap . He aimed to carry out the administrative work without any error and for the benefit of his subjects. He shaped the future of Patayat Late Nursingha Pratap, gave him a good education, and assigned him the most respectable position in the king's court. As an elder brother, King Shankar Pratap thought that Patayat brother will carry on the work of the king's court in a proper way. But in the absence of the king and without his knowledge many unfavorable things against the administration were done so Patayat Nursingha Pratap was removed from the administrative work. He left his house and property in Dhenkanal and left. Sometimes he visited Dhenkanal to look after it.

King Shankar Pratap's administration was an amalgamation of expert, highly educated, hardworking, and responsible people. He and his administrators gave their best. His aim was to establish his state as the best state. On both side of the stairs of the palace there were two boxes. One of the boxes had a green cover and the other one had a red cover. One was meant to receive the appeal application of the general public and the other one was to receive the complaint regarding the administrative activities and unjust. He personally looked into the complaints and carried out the proceedings. I am attaching the rules of the Dhenkanal state of that time in Annexure- II.

Dhenkanal's royal family's traditional decorum was to selflessly devote them and to carry out their responsibilities. No one from the royal family tried to gain name and fame and to be known as a memorable person by showing self-pride or by donating. According to their capability, they took the literate, hardworking and brave people from their territory and appointed them as the soldiers, trained them, and took their help to keep the border safe. In the history, you will find the description of the bravery and the warfare techniques of the Dhenkanal soldiers. In the war, the soldiers of Dhenkanal were never defeated as they showed their courage, valor, and warfare technique. At all times they were victorious and helped in expanding the Dhenkanal state.

The victory was not only limited to the king rather it was the victory of the king's army. In other words, it was the victory of the people as the people representatives were appointed. It is a pride for both the king and his subjects. Dhenkanal's royal family was able to spread its boundary with its strength and knowledge but never tried to overpower the people of the state by misusing the power.

He never tried to involve himself in the judicial matter. Never gave the death sentence rather gave direction to the state administration to follow truth, compassion, and justice while carrying out the administrative work. Everything depends on trust.

King Shankar Pratap trusted the chieftain and the watchman of the villages and considered them as a part of the administration and respected them. Because of this faith and trust, the watchmen of the villages received little land without taxes as a salary and rendered their work. Their service for the people was to safeguard them. Though they were untouchable but to get minimum wages and a little tax free land they worked day and night, performed their duty lawfully and neutrally, and were accepted in the mainstream of the king's administration. The watchmen never gave judgment or order.

Whatever power was assigned to them, they used it fearlessly in the appropriate place at appropriate time and all of them accepted it as a part of the administration. If a new person visits the village whether his activity is suspicious or not was watched by the watchman and was reported. They remain awake in the night and kept a watch over the village.

They reported regarding the fights in the village, quarrels, forest protection, attendance of the children in the school, absence of the teachers in the school, theft, destruction of the crops, the rage of the wild animals, murder, tumult because of drinking, social activities, and festivals and tried to maintain peace, law, and order. During any investigation the witness of the village watchman was acceptable. In the village, the watchman helped the nongovernmental registered organizations in their work. As a result all the details of the village, right from farming to the business, how are the villagers related, how are they interested, and how far it's stretched was reported immediately by the village watchman in the king's court. What is the state of farming, how much loss has been incurred because of the destruction of crops by flood and famine, how is the income from the crop all these details reached the king's court instantly.

According to this information, the necessary action was taken. That's why the king's administration could run smoothly with limited revenue. Because of the governing body and watchman arrangement system, theft, destruction of crops, fights, quarrels, and anti social activities mostly didn't happen in the villages. Though there was sorrow and pain because of poverty still people lead a fearless life. There was good cooperation among people.

The governing body of the village was the steer man in the actual sense. Though they didn't have the power of an administrator, but they worked as appointed approved social representatives according to the instructions and order of the king's court. To maintain law and order in the village, Pucca house management, the maintenance of the public property, collaboration with the government employees, helping them in their work, protection of forest and village resources, festivals, maintenance of the temples, arrangements for the guests, arrangement for farming, collection of revenue, etc were done flawlessly and perfectly by them as non-governmental employees.

They were always hospitable. They devoted their time for the progress of the village. They didn't get the salary, but received honor from the king's court and love and affection of the people. They didn't expect for anything and worked for the progress of their village. They thought that was their prime duty. In case of any occurrence or mishap, they gave their views and suggestion regarding it to the administrator. Proper steps were taken according to that. In this process injustice, corruption, bribery, and other occurrences didn't happen in the villages. King Shankar Pratap considered them as a part of the administration and trusted them. He didn't tolerate anyone troubling them or disrespecting them.

It's about one of the incidents. The revenue collector of a village came to deposit the revenue collected from the tax. At that time the tax was collected in two instalments and the rolling currency was tanka, adhuli, suuki, ana, and paisa. As compared to the British administration areas and other states, the tax was less in Dhenkanal. The amount that the village revenue collector brought in that tanka, adhuli, and suuki was less. Ana, paisa, adhuli, and pahula was more. It was counted and kept in a gunny bag and was brought by a man on his shoulder. There was no proper transport facility at that time. So they walked and reached Dhenkanal in the evening and stayed in Gujuri Hata.

At present, it is converted to Indira market. It was an open house with a tin shed. Every day hata was organized and many people came to that place for selling vegetables and other essential goods. They stay there and cook for themselves. After their work is over they leave the place. There was no fear of theft. No one bossed over others rather they had respect for each other and were hospitable. The next day the village revenue collector completed his daily chores and before the administrative work started he went to deposit the tax money. The person who will count the money and give the receipt with the seal asked whether he had brought tanka and adhuli or has brought paisa, adhalaa, and pahulaa.

The village revenue collector said very politely how will he get tanka and adhuli? The way the tax is imposed on the public in that case paisa, adhula and pahula is more. The tax collector said, 'I don't have time to count this. Separate it the tanka and adhula or it will be reported to the king.' The staff spoke to him rudely, got busy in some other work and didn't keep the tax money. He threatened the village administrator that he will report to the king regarding it and he will be punished as he brought paisa, adhula and pahula. Raja Sahib didn't know that. Even if he comes to know how can he punish him for bringing paisa, adhula and pahula? But the concerned staff told this to the village revenue collector and tried to scare him and also didn't accept the money which he brought. The poor fellow waited there for a long time and as his request wasn't heard he went back to the Gujuri Hata with the gunny bag to spend the night. In this way, two days passed.

He went back to the same person again on the third day and requested him to keep the money. He also said that the food grain which he had brought along with him is over so he can't stay there for a long time and requested him to accept the tax money.

The person who was collecting the tax very cleverly told him that he will help him. He asked,' Is there is any remaining instalment of the tax to be deposited? How much money is there in the bag?' The answer was the bag has the exact amount which is required to be deposited. He asked, 'How much extra amount do you have?' The revenue collector's answer was, 'Whatever money I brought with me is already spent as I had to stay here for three days and today I don't have money to eat. I have to starve today or have to go back.' The staff very coolly said, 'Give me some money from the tax amount. The amount which you give me, include the same amount in the pending amount for the next.

Next time when you deposit, add that amount. If it's acceptable I will count the money or I will start doing some other work. The revenue collector thought it's better to accept this proposal rather than to be in a problem as he has to stay back for few more days there and have to starve or have to take back the money and return to his village. Of course, he has to give an explanation regarding the pending amount but that can be done later. At present, it's necessary to get rid of this situation.

On the third day, the counting began. Right from the beginning till the end a treasury guard was watching and listening to the conversation. Around 1 pm the treasury guard after his duty went back to his home which was in the police compound. He saw Raja Sahib sitting alone. He saluted Raja Sahib and Raja Sahib asked him what's going on around him. The police guard was very much hurt by the way the revenue collector was troubled. He narrated to Raja Sahib everything in detail right from the beginning till the end.

The revenue collector was called by the king. He was asked many questions like when did he come, why did he come, what's the situation in the village, how is the farming going on, about education and his work. The king asked him everything in detail. He also asked whether the tax was collected forcefully or the people gave it peacefully. Then he came to the real issue which he wanted to discuss with the revenue collector and he unwilling told the truth to Raja Sahib.

The particular staff was called to meet Raja Sahib. He asked him seriously in a heavy voice, 'Do you know this person?' The reply was 'Yes'. He asked the man,' Why didn't you keep the tax amount from him for three days and troubled him?' The king said, 'The tax money which is collected by them is deposited in the treasury and people like us get the salary from that amount for our living. Is it not treacherous to trouble a person like him rather than showing him respect?' You have to amend your act. Tell me how you will give him back his lost respect? He ordered him to go away from his sight immediately. King Shankar Pratap, the powerful and sovereign king, with a clean heart, in a calm and composed voice, in a regretful manner, begged pardon from the revenue collector. Is it not the kindness of the king?

Few selfish people, for their personal gain, tried to spread the illusion to exploit and trouble the poor and illiterate people. They always tried to plot schemes but they couldn't succeed in their aim because of King Shankar Pratap. These rattle brained people always criticized the king and became his foes. The question arises why didn't a powerful king like him ordered for the death sentence or banishment to these parasitic people?

He could have done this, he had the power according to the prevailing rules and regulations but King Shankar Pratap never thought of punishing anyone in this way on the other hand he was fair and strict in his judgment. There was no doubt about it. Our contribution to get independence isn't less. Those who blame the kings in history, they know very well directly or indirectly that the contribution of the kings wasn't less. They initiated the national movement in their own way. Independence is there in their blood and it's in their lineage. They never accepted anyone overpowering them. They understood the real meaning of dignity and independence so they never looked back. They sacrificed their lives to achieve it. They knew how to achieve it and how to use it properly to enhance the value of life.

My childhood was moulded as per the culture and heritage of Sareikela but it developed to its fullest after my marriage with King Shankar Pratap. He had the power to mold others into a dignified person. He proved himself as an ideal son, ideal husband, ideal father, ideal brother, ideal guardian, and an ideal ruler in every field of life. He helped me enhance my limited knowledge as an ideal husband and this has helped me in my arena of work in the latter part of my life. I could get rid of the fear as a woman because of his teachings. I got the power to face the problem boldly and to settle it only because of his inspiration.

I was able to decipher the truth from many occurrences because of his compassion. He was not only my life partner but was the most reverend and respectful person in my life, my role model, and a pathfinder of my life. His thoughts, his spiritual life, and his ideology helped me and shape me as an ideal woman in Indian society. I could shape myself as an inspirational wife, affectionate sister, and a mother. It's my good luck. Sometimes the old memories of life weave the thread in the woof.

It is meaningful, educative and content of history. There is no exaggeration in it. I am narrating a true story which is written in the Vidhan Sabha report. The place of discussion was Vidhan Sabha. In the year 1965, in the month of March during the budget session there was a discussion in Vidhan Sabha. In that session the discussion was regarding establishment of Science college in Dhenkanal, land reformation, flood related disaster and how to curb it, Panchayat confederation ,women education and establishing a women's college in Dhenkanal , about torture in jail, famine, watchman appointment practice, health, forest, water supply, farming equipments, and distribution of control ration and various other things.

At that time I was elected from the Dhenkanal constituency from the Independent party and was a MLA. As Congress lost from my constituency and other Gadajat areas the government didn't do any developmental works in these areas. What was the reason for not doing developmental work was not known. As the public had complete faith and trust in us so they allowed us to represent them right from the year 1957 till date.

Dhenkanal's public is hardworking and truthful. They can break but can never bend or kneel in front of others for their selfish gains. They never compromised their independence. Those who tried to betray them, the people of Dhenkanal retaliated against them fiercely. They never accepted any ones sympathy, pity, or alms rather they tried to protect their rights with the ethics of struggle in life. We the royal family whole heartedly accepted this strategy of the people of Dhenkanal and worked accordingly to keep their fundamental values intact.

In this regard- in the legislative assembly, in the presence of the entire elected member on 13.03.1975, I in my speech mentioned it in a very emotional way that I am a 'Mother'. As a mother, I have equal duty for everyone. Whatever problems I saw, I mentioned there. I told them that along with my district, I wish for the development of other 12 districts. The ruling party and the opposition party were impressed by that and they praised me for my general and   service oriented ideology. The other members were also influenced by this. When a member thinks about the benefit of only his constituency it tells about the narrow-mindedness of that person and it's not appreciated.

King Shankar Pratap unnecessarily didn't interfere

in the administrative work. He could easily assess whether the work was done properly by the person to whom it's assigned or not because of his experience. He gave his valuable suggestions and feedbacks whenever it was required. He also showed the person the right path and guided him and even after that if it wasn't possible for the person to do so, he tried guide the person in such a way that in every field the person was able to prove himself.

He had a deep faith in me. He discussed with me regarding the state administration and also regarding other personal issues. He even sought my opinion and advice. He never took the decision without seeking any opinion or without discussion. There were no issues in taking his own decision himself but, to know others opinion, to evaluate others knowledge, to know about others judgmental capability, he involved everyone in the discussion. He appreciated the contradiction and he believed in the strength of others. The only reason behind it was, he was knowledgeable, clean hearted, benignant, principled, virtuous, and was modernistic.

I followed his ideology. To help King Shankar Pratap in his administrative work I was appointed as the chairman of the endowment department. I was not paid for it but the job had lots of responsibilities. He had the faith that I had the capability to manage the endowment work along with my own personal responsibilities so he entrusted me with this work. Though I was a little worried still I made myself mentally strong and was determined to achieve success in this work and to prove myself. In the beginning, he kept track of whether I am regularly attending the office or not like the other employees. He discussed with me regarding the every day's program and the procedures as a result my efficiency in doing the work enhanced and the work in the endowment department could be carried out smoothly.

Among the temples in Dhenkanal are, Kapilash, Shri Shri Chandrasekhar temple, Shri Shri Balaram Jew temple, Panchameswara, Nadhara Ramchandi, Saptasajya's Raghunath Jew temple, Nagnath temple, Dadhibamana temple. Other than these temples there are many Mahadev temples and temples of other gods and goddesses. There are also Grama Debata and Grama Devi in the villages. With the help of the royal family and the people, these institutions were constructed at various times in various places to mitigate spirituality.

It was not only because of the belief in God but because of the faith in the Almighty which prevailed and is still prevailing. Right from the reign of the Late King Nurshigha Bidyadhara till Kamakhya Prasad Singh Deo at different times various temples were constructed. The construction work of Saptasajya's Raghunath Jew temple began under King Shankar Pratap and my supervision and our son Kamakhya Prasad, after the death of King Shankar Pratap brought the idol, performed the Vedic rituals, and placed the idol in the temple. For the daily rituals of God from our side land has been allotted.

Dhenkanal's royal family's descent wasn't only the construction of the temple and installation of idols in the temple. It wasn't limited to that. They spent their life with faith and belief in God and spirituality. They also helped in the consecration of Madrasa, Masjid, Tajia, and Mahima Dharma. They donated many tax free lands for the temples and for conducting the fairs and festivals. Even the arrangements were made for the proper functioning of the Grama Devi temples in the villages by donating tax free land. In those fields' vegetables, grains, cereals, and sugarcane were grown and were used for various purposes in the temple. Therefore for the daily rituals of God the temple authority didn't depend on anyone.

In few places milk, ghee, and curd were also supplied. Where ever there was a tradition of sacrifice, the goats were reared. Other than these to solve the financial problem, the endowment department extended the financial help during the fairs and festivals.

The kings of this royal family wouldn't have created the endowment department and would have kept the temple rituals in their hands but they didn't do that. If they would have done so the ego in them would have increased, they would have gained control and there would have been self-interest. They never thought that the temples belong to them and gave the rights to the general public to do the worship so that everyone will have a sense of belongingness. When we look at that, it can be said that it was a distinctive broad perspective and representation of a glorious and balanced society.

In Dhenkanal's royal family the kings visited the temples and prayed to the gods and goddesses regularly before beginning any work. They performed the rituals in a properly. The kings of the family were inclined towards spirituality so they were benevolent, forgiving, generous, lawful, and secular.

They didn't rule with illusion neither cared for denunciation nor were exhilarated by praise. They were visionaries, imagined about the future and thought about the past. They were realistic, industrious, and not pretentious. All these good qualities were found in them because of the god's grace. Keeping this in view, they not only constructed the temples for the public but also made arrangements for their proper functioning with the help of the endowment department.

The priests of the temple made their living out of this. The guests could get the Prasad easily. The poor people could get Prasad with very little money. Many people were engaged in cultivating the land that was given to God and made their living. Even though the earning was less still they could manage. Other than that the fairs and festivals were celebrated with pomp and show to inculcate spirituality among people. Along with that few entertainment programs were also arranged. At that time people enjoyed this according to their likes and dislikes. The shops were also set up in the fair for the sell and purchase of daily use goods .As a result, there was an increase in the business and people could also get the daily necessities. It was a necessary part of social life.

After I took the charge of the endowment department, I first tried to understand the ritual of the god and goddesses, method of worship, the offerings to the god, about the lands, about the harvest, its protection, and utility. I also tried to learn about the barn and its protection. I could gain knowledge about the endowment work and after, that I could do my work flawlessly without any problem. I visited the barns and temples and gathered the information regarding the ritual timing, about the offerings to the god, protection of the property, and other related works and analysed them. Other than that I enquired about the stay of the travellers those who have come to visit the temple, about their wellbeing and food. I tried to solve the problem if any and tried to maintain the law and order. I gave a lot of importance to cleanliness in the temples.

To keep the environment clean and green, trees and plants were planted and were taken care of. The rituals of the god and goddesses were performed in a traditional way keeping in mind the sanctity of it and in a religious manner. The appointed priests and other people were instructed to do their work judiciously. I always insisted them to behave in a dignified way. That's why there was no mistake found in any field. Where ever there were barns in the name of the god, the fields were self-cultivated. If any misuse or unnecessary expenditure was brought to my notice during my visit, it was immediately rectified. Where ever the tenant farming was done, I visited those places also.

The farmer is doing the farming properly or not, whether the income is good or not, whether the land is taken care of properly or not, the harvest is low or high, if less than what's the reason behind it, all these things were supervised by me with a lot of enthusiasm and care. That's why the tenant farmers did the farming properly and kept their portion and deposited the rest to be used for the rituals of the god in the temple treasury. In the case of lease farming, the same thing was applied.

Therefore there was no deviation in the rituals of the god, in the protection of property, and the Darshan of the devotees and the patrons. These places of worship were a place which gave immense peace and were also places of great importance. All of them in the endowment department were happy with my work. King Shankar Pratap Singh Deo kept an eye on my work with and without my knowledge and was happy that I was working dedicatedly. I carried out the work assigned to me by him flawlessly and efficiently. He wasn't only happy rather felt proud and said that in a male dominated rigid society of India, a woman like me could do the administrative work successfully and could show the potential, efficiency, devotion, secularism, and courage. I was glorified. Though

I felt proud of it but I always remembered and accepted that I gained knowledge from him, I am a traveller in his shown path. I achieved success in all my endeavours but, it was his achievement, not mine.

The glorious lineage's dignified men bore the notion of devotee and devotion and constructed the temples at various times for the general public. Arrangements were made for the proper functioning of these temples by allotting movable and immovable property. All of them had the right to worship and to take part in the fairs and festivals. Though the kings took care of all but for the general public, it was a place of worship. There was no controversy regarding this as it was accepted by everyone as a pious place. It was a place of social, spiritual, and cultural development. It was also accepted as a place of economic development unanimously. Keeping this as the base and the faith of everyone, devotional, social activities and farming related activities was done.

Today it is discussed about socialism and solidarity at that time irrespective of caste, creed, and religion these institutions were established. The discrimination that is created according to caste, creed, and religion is created by some selfish minded people for their own benefit and those are the people who scream and screech about racial discrimination. The face of politics and administration has changed for these types of people. The eighty crore population of India is still burning in this fire. Before the independence in the areas under the reign of the kings and Nawabs, there was a lot of discrimination according to caste, creed, and religion. Sometimes it happened because of the conspiracy of the British administration not because of the people and the Indian rulers, but it was projected as the indifference that is caused due to the caste, creed, and religion and the hard core thoughts of the community.

Such type of incident never happened in Odisha during our time. Where there is good understanding, there is affection and equality; such disgraceful things never take place there. During the court administration in Dhenkanal, there were no differences created taking into account the caste, creed, and religion and no one thought about it. All of them celebrated their fairs and festivals happily and also rendered their help to make the necessary arrangements. Tajia went around the town and also came to the palace. We also did the needful. During Lakshmi Puja each and every community rendered their help. Today we can see chaos in society, financial problems, political issues, degradation of character, less productivity, extinction of age old culture. It has only happened because of the sheer negligence towards the religious institutions and it's true.

Dhenkanal's endowment department was under my supervision. I still remember my experience during my work in the department. The way I was brought up and I have spent my life; I still have the enthusiasm to visit religious places. I have the faith that by performing the rituals of the god life becomes complete. But today when I visit the temples and see it ache my heart. A place that was pious, sacred, and clean has turned into an untidy place.

The place has lost its sanctity because of the ungrateful people. The atmosphere is disturbed. The unjust, ruthlessness, and self-interest activities have created a fear to visit these places.

Dhenkanal's endowment department's main trustee is district collector. According to his instructions, all the proceedings were carried out in the endowment department. For the protection of the land under the settlement and farming, agricultural experts, and employees are appointed. Other than that the advisors, amina, landlords and many other employees are appointed for the smooth functioning of the department. A vehicle is also available to travel.

Despite of all these, it can be said that the department doesn't have a record of all the institutions and property in Dhenkanal. What's the state of the land, where is it and in what condition, is it in records or not, has anyone grabbed the land forcefully, what is the production capacity of the land, and does a part of it comes to the treasury meant for god, this type of things are kept secretly by the department or maybe they don't have an idea about it. In a similar way, how are the trees, ponds, and groves used and by whom are they used, whether the revenue comes to the treasury meant for god, no one knows that. In many places, people have made the false land documents in their names though it belongs to the endowment department. The department doesn't have any knowledge about it nor is interested to take any steps against it. The vehicle isn't used to supervise the barns and the agricultural lands.

In spite of the available vehicle, the endowment department goes forward to rent a vehicle. At present to include the property in the endowment record no such plans are made. No steps are taken to bring a change in the mismanagement. It seems the functioning of the religious institutions is confined to the whims and fancies of the endowment department. Is it possible? Everything is coming to an end. Nothing will be left out at the end. Things can be rectified. Hard work and commitment is required for that. No one can get spared by the wrath of God. Society will regret it.

If God is satisfied the poor will get food to eat. If a

lamp is lightened in the temple it will evade the darkness in the society. With the fumes of the incense stick, the atmosphere will get purified. Despite of a literate and educated person being in the endowment department, if the work isn't done in a proper way it will lead to disaster. When they don't have any contribution to increasing the temple property then do they have any right to destroy it?

The present situation of the temples is because of the rules that were made by the ruling administrators. Their intention has landed all of them in a problem. That's why society is degrading now. They have lost their prudence because of poverty. The atmosphere is filled with lamentation. As the people of our country are religious, they believe that the condition in our country is deteriorating because of their negligence towards God. Adulterated food as prasad and adulterated ghee is served to God. No proper timing is followed for the rituals and the free prasad is sold at a high price.

Previously the work of the endowment department was appreciated by everyone and we did the work with sanctity. To misuse the property which belongs to God is an unrighteous act, we believed in that which today's administration has completely consigned to oblivion. I wish that the mismanagement stops, they start thinking wisely, let there be a healthy resolution to this issue and there be better management.

I wasn't only associated with the endowment department but also with the state's Health Department. Women health care was under my supervision. King Shankar Pratap appointed a lady doctor for the first time after consulting me. As a lady doctor was appointed so the woman folk came for their treatment without any apprehensions and fear and were benefited. A separate female ward was constructed and it started functioning. I supervised the treatment of the patients, distribution of the medicines, the cleanliness of the hospital, and the surrounding.

As a result, the patients were comfortable and were happy. The hospital employees were also very much devoted to their work and their aim was to work for the patients. There was no chance of taking the money from the patients in an illogical way. I was also a part of the discussion regarding the other administrative work other than the work entrusted to me. My opinion and advice was solicited. Most of the time my opinion was legitimate and it was accepted.

King Shankar Pratap recollected the history or the things that happened in the past and accepted the positive things in a similar way he could very well judge the things that are going to happen in the future and about its repercussion. It was one of his inborn qualities. He had predicted that the efforts that the people of India are putting to get independence, after independence people will go through many problems and suffer and will put a lot more effort to come out of it. He felt sad while discussing this.

He stated that there will be indifferences between caste, creed, and religion, between states and it will take a frightful shape. He also said that because of the freedom and narrow mindedness among the political leaders the atmosphere will become noxious. As a result, poverty will increase, there will be health hazards, and people will mourn for their ill fate. Whatever he told was accurate. Still, we couldn't resolve this problem rather it's becoming more and more complicated and one problem gives rise to many problems.

Right from the differences between Hindu and Muslim, the construction of Ram Mandir in Ayodhya,

Punjab, Kashmir, and Naga problems there are endless problems from one end to the other end of the country. There is also political rivalry which has ravaged the country's financial and social condition in every sphere. The anarchy and lawlessness are increasing day by day and that's the reason why the country is still in a developing stage and can't be counted as a developed nation. The unscrupulous leaders sing their own praise, try their best to allure people, and take them on an erroneous path.

King Shankar Pratap was a selfless patriot who was ethical and righteous. He was far sighted, knowledgeable, and organized. He did his work after analyzing his thoughts logically. That's why his judgment was always impeccable. He had set an example for others because of his work ethic. His opinion was solicited while taking decisions regarding political and administrative work. He had a solution to each and every problem. All were satisfied because of this. He could save the state from many troubles during difficult situations. It was an example of his wisdom. He is immortal.

British government handed over the freedom of this country to the Indian politicians on 15, August 1947. But to break the unity and integrity of the country they showed the poisonous seed of feud and that has taken a dreadful shape. That was consternation for the people of this country. There is no resolution to this and all are sufferers.

According to the British rule of that time, the states which were ruled by the kings were supposed to get amalgamated. As a large sovereign independent country when India started building up its foundation, at that time to give a complete substantial shape to the country wasn't wrong. If history is analysed, many facts come into the light, but it was analysed according to the convenience of the leaders which can't be counted as a part of history.

In the year 1947, on 13 December, India's Deputy Prime Minister, the Iron Man of India Sardar Vallabhbhai Patel came to Cuttack to discuss about the integration of the princely states into India and organized a meeting of the kings. There were many things which were discussed in the meeting. During this discussion, many justifiable proposals were raised by the kings. To bring those proposals within the mandate and to execute it was a difficult task. Sardar Patel was a strong willed and determined person. He was a lawyer so he didn't accept the things which deviated from the law and constitutional rights. On that day, in the afternoon, during the break, Sardar Patel consulted his old friend King Shankar Pratap.

Sardar Patel during the discussion said, if anyone can settle this matter in a proper may with unanimous consent, he is King Shankar Pratap. That proved to be right. In the second half of the session, during the discussion King Shankar Pratap, gave an example of his patriotism and answered the difficult questions that were raised in the meeting and also motivated others to renounce their personal interest and to think about the prosperity of the country. His arguments didn't break the law to a certain extent but were persuasive. King Shankar Pratap was the one who first approved the integration of the princely states and signed on the proposal. This is a part of the glorious history.

The Secretary to Indian government Shri V.P Menon in his book vividly mentioned regarding this. Can there be any other example of King Shankar Pratap's self introduction other than this? The integration of the princely state with Odisha was only possible at that time because of King Shankar Pratap's leadership.

The agreement which was made between the kings

regarding their fundamental rights ,that wasn't suspended or denied because at that time the constitution wasn't formed in India as a sovereign country and by introducing new amendments in law what to suspend and what to accept wasn't determined. Among the public few credible persons those who were knowledgeable had individuality and were influential along with few kings gave a proposal for a new independent state named 'Maha Kaushal'. It wasn't irrelevant according to the situation at that time. It was said that it may cause a hindrance in the formation of Odisha as a large state. But if the 'Maha Kaushal' state would have been created then the Odiya speaking areas which were in Bihar, Madhya Pradesh, Andhra Pradesh, and Bengal would have been included in this and the people would have got an opportunity to stay freely and independently in their language spoken state. At present, also many Odiya language spoken areas are under different states and the people are still devoid of their rights.

Another reason was along with Sambalpur many princely states were rich in minerals and forest resources but compared to Mugalbandi areas they weren't developed. Though they had the manpower but they didn't get the opportunity to develop. The British administration collected the revenue from the princely states and after that whatever was left from the revenue was used for the developmental purpose.

British rulers collected the revenue but never gave any grant for the developmental purpose. They collected revenue from the kings on various pretext and used that revenue for the developmental work of their directly ruled Mugalbandi areas. Schools, colleges, hospitals, and many other institutions were constructed from the revenue collected from the princely states in Mugalbadi areas. So comparatively the princely states were far behind. That was the reason why Maha Kaushal state formation was suggested so that by using the available natural and forest resources the state can develop like the Mugalbadi areas.

The necessity of this is realized today by the people. At that time King Shankar Pratap very firmly raised his voice and said that it is necessary to bring together all the Odiya spoken areas which are in other states and to make a sole Odisha and that is what is expected. For this reason, the cooperation and effort of all is solicited. It is disheartening that according to his vision all the Odiya speaking areas couldn't be brought together. After the integration of the princely states, it was necessary to form Odisha state. Odisha couldn't be formed as a big state because of the infirm leadership of the political leaders. In every field, King Shankar Pratap's brilliance was reflected. He never paid attention to hearsay, kept himself away from pretenders and narrow minded people, and never showed false vanity.

From the year 1947 to 1951 the Interim Government of India was formed. Jawaharlal Nehru was the Prime Minister in the centre. Dr. Harekrushna Mahatab was the Chief Minister in Odisha. In the year 1950, 26 January constitution of India came into effect thus, turning the nation into a newly formed republic. In the year 1957 was the second general election. King Shankar Pratap and I contested in the general election from Dhenkanal and Kamakhya Nagar constituency. As the voters of Dhenkanal had a deep faith in us so we won the election. King Shankar Pratap got 29970 votes and I got 20784 votes and got elected. In the year 1961, I contested with Biju Patnaik and won the election by 5000 votes.

In the year 1961 Gana parishad was a state level party. That year it got merged in the Swatantra party. King

Shankar Pratap Singh Deo Mahendra Bahadur was chosen as the candidate from Swatantra party to contest for the parliament seat in the year 1962 and in this election, Shri Baishnab Charan Patnaik defeated him in many votes and was elected. In the year 1964 my husband was elected to Rajya Sabha and in the year 1965 in our Calcutta residence, 14, Camac Street he breathed his last. He left me and my children mourning. At that time Samaj and Hindustan Standard published about his demise. Harekrushna Mahatab sent his condolence letter. The letter and my son Patayat Matru Prasad Singh Deo's written 'Pitru Smaran' is detailed in Annexure III.

In the year 1965 Odisha was under the clutches of famine and at that time many opposition leaders did the agitation movement. In Vidhan Sabha, the opposition leader Shri Rajendra Narayan Singh Deo and in Lok Sabha the king of Kalahandi and Lok Sabha member Shri Pratap Keshari Deo presented the motion respectively and did many famine eradication related programs.

The 4th general election was held in the year 1967 in which Lok Sabha and Rajya Sabha election were included. At that time in spite of my unwillingness, my brother Shri Rajendra Narayan Singh Deo who was Odisha Vidhan Sabha's opposition party leader tried to make me understand to contest in the election keeping in mind my late husband King Shankar Pratap's incomplete work to be completed and to serve the people of Dhenkanal. In the 1967 election only seven contestants contested. Among them was Dhenkanal parliament constituency's Shri Baishnab Charan Patanaik, Dhenkanal's voters elected me with a lot of votes and the other seven contestants lost. Along with me, my son Kamakhya Prasad Sigh Deo was also elected as the MP from the Dhenkanal constituency. For the first time, the cabinet was formed which was non Congress and Shri Rajendra Narayan Sigh Deo became the Chief Minister.

King Shankar Pratap proved himself as a representative of the people in Vidhan Sabha and Rajya Sabha because of his multifaceted personality. He persuaded the government for the developmental work for the people by his cogent arguments. As an example, to give an appointment to the literate unemployed youth in the Rourkela Steel plant King Shankar Pratap passed the Private Members bill in Rajya Sabha and it was accepted unanimously. It is a historic step in the parliamentary procedure.

In the year 1958-59 Raja Sahib ,I and Belatikiri Grama Panchayat's sarpancha of that time and Odisha Vidhan Sabha's former member Shri Haladhar Mishra ,by the invitation of Indian government's minister Shri S.K Dey went to participate in the All India party development camp orientation course held at Mussoorie. After we came back, I along with King Shankar Pratap went to the villages, tribal areas, mountain regions, and forest areas. Till his last breath, King Shankar Pratap kept himself involved in this party development work and as a member of Rajya Sabha discussed along with the local representatives and the government employees about their respective areas and advised them. Though he was in the opposition party still no one could overlook his proposal.

Whatever work is done in Dhenkanal till date, the foundation of all those was laid by him. Later on it was possible to execute those work because of groundwork was already done by him. He could flawlessly present the problems of the people. The center of the ancient Kalinga, Utkala, and at present Odisha ,its history ,art, culture, literature, politics, social, and economy is Shreekshetra

Puri's Lord Jagannath, Jagannath culture and Gajapati Maharaja. His influence is far and wide irrespective of caste, creed, and religion. Ancient Kalinga, Utkala or today's Odisha's rise and fall isn't only centred around Lord Jagannath and its culture but also the rise and fall of the whole nation are centred around it. This can't be denied. Only because of deep faith in Lord Jagannath and Jagannath Sanskriti, and being influenced by Jagannath dharma his main valet, worshipper, and devotee Gajapati Maharaja could make the state as an acclaimed state. Of course, there was a rise and fall but they didn't lose their originality and didn't accept any one's subjection.

They proved themselves as the ideal community in every field. Once upon a time with the blessings of Lord Jagannath the army of Gajapati Maharaja spread the kingdom from Ganga to Godavari. His incomparable strength and power existed for a long time in this country. Because of this reason the British government who had the modern warfare technique couldn't capture Odisha. They tried their best by using their power, knowledge, and craft but still couldn't overpower the Odiya clan. The British government applied its political chicanery with the help of a few disloyal traitors and indigene and captured Kalinga, Utkala or, today's Odisha. The pride, courage, and valour of the people of Odisha are recorded in the history.

In this way, with a supreme pride, ancient Kalinga, Utkala, or Odisha's spiritual, political, and social leadership had acceptance from many other kings, administrators, and individual person. The people from every region of India are devoted to Lord Jagannath, they show their respect and reverence for Jagannath culture , and Gajapati Maharaja. Because of this reason, many saints, administrators, and devotees from various parts of India came to Shreekshetra for Jagannath darshan, to know about Jagannath Sanskriti, or to see Gajapati Maharaja. Though it's a story from the past but it's a historical truth without any doubt.

At that time Jharkhand or Jharkhand region was a princely state. This region was full of forests and mountains and was inaccessible. The region had fewer inhabitants and was full of wild animals. The people were simple, brave, and independent. They weren't literate and were conservative but they lived an independent and free life. They worked hard and made their living from farming and forest resources. Among them, there were few small kings but they believed in Lord Jagannath and had respect for Gajapati Maharaja and accepted him. The illiterate people of Jharkhand region at many times seek for the help of Gajapati Maharaja.

At many times many intellectual people came to Shreekshetra for Jagannath darshan and showed their knowledge, potential, capability, and devotion according to its utility in a respectable manner to gain the favour of Gajapati Maharaja.

I have a deep bond with Dhenkanal in my life that will remain incomplete if I don't write few lines about the history of the royal family of Dhenkanal. But before writing this I thought it is necessary to consult few experienced writers and historians. Among them was my brother in law Ninibhai Rajkumar Shri Sesha Pratap Singh Deo, Shri Rudranarayan Mishra, Shri Ranendra Pratap Singh Deo, Shri Rajiblochan Singh Deo, Shri Krushnachandra Harichandan Sigh, Shri Surendra Mishra, and Shri Chandra Mohan. Other than these people Shri Ramachandra Nanda Bhakti Binoda's written "Dhenkanal's History" was of much help.

Chapter- V

DHENKANAL'S ROYAL FAMILY AND THEIR ADMINISTRATION

Dhenkanal's royal family came into existence in the year 1530. The founder of this family was the primeval man Hari Singh Bidyadhara. Hari Singh Bidyadhara who was a Kshatriya came on a visit to Puri and it came to his knowledge that Gajapati Maharaja with an intention to conquer the south is on the war front. He took the advantage of this and fought bravely against the Southern region king on behalf of Gajapati Maharaja Pratap Rudradeb. He defeated the Southern region king and brought his turban, sword, and symbol which was an image of victory, and presented it to Gajapati Maharaja. Gajapati Maharaj Pratap Rudradeb was astonished by the bravery and might show by Hari Singh and arranged for a special court to honour him.

In that court, he gave Hari Singh Bidyadhar Karamula Patana of Jharkhand and gave him the rights to rule over it. The symbols like the turban, sword, and minaketan which he brought after defeating the Southern king and was presented to Gajapati Maharaja those symbols were given to him during his coronation by Gajapati Maharaj and he told him to make those as his state symbol. This Karamula is at present near Mahima Dharma Pitha Joranda, in Karamula Panchayat in the banks of the river Brahmani in Aswakhola mountain region. At present, the ravages of it exist and the artistically engraved Ganesh idol is still worshipped there.

In order to establish himself as the mightiest king, Karamula Patana's king Hari Singh Bidyadhara started working on it right after his coronation. He started organizing many programs of political confederation in his state. Among this was to form the state army and to train them. To gain the confidence of the people he also started many delightful programs. The people very honestly in an open heart accepted King Hari Singh Bidyadhar as their king. Slowly the people showed their respect, devotion, and attachment towards him. King Hari Singh Bidyadhar took advantage of this and continued his reign. At that time he could easily bring the small states under his control because of his power, intellect, and attractive government activities.

As a result, his state boundary expanded and he could prove himself as a mighty king and along with that because of his good governance he became popular. He started to expand his reign towards the south and at present, nearer to Dhenkanal fort, defeated Beshaliya fort's Bhanja dynasty king and after capturing Dhenkanal he realized the importance of the place and thought this place to be safe from all aspects in the foothills of Pani Ohala Mountain and he constructed the fort there.

The Bhanja dynasty king was defeated and before his death, he told about the curse of "Dhenkasabara". He told along with Dhenkasabara few small states of Nali will be combined and named as Dhenkanal and it was a request by Dhenkasabar King to Bhanja king. King Hari Singh

Bidyadhar accepted it. A stone which was named as Dhenkasabar head is still worshipped on a particular day in a year according to the Sabar rituals.

From the year 1530 King Hari Singh Bidyadhar to expand his territory was engaged in war with many small states. After his victory over other small states he was busy with his state's administrative work as a result he didn't find time to visit Shreekshetra Puri for the darshan till 1594. Though many years passed, still his respect and reverence for Gajapati Maharaja didn't lessen. His devotion and faith towards Lord Jagannath, Balabhadra, and Subhadra were becoming stronger and stronger day by day. In the year 1594 King Hari Singh Bidyadhar went to Puri for darshan. Gajapati Maharaja with due respect had made special arrangements for the king of Dhenkanal for Jagganath darshan. Since that day till now Dhenkanal's royal family has got the privilege and facility to go for Lord Jagganath darshan .

King Hari Singh Bidyadhar constructed his fort in Dhenkanal. The construction of Balaram temple is one of his glories. He tried his best to make Kapilash's Chandrashekhar temple a renowned pilgrimage. He brought the Kula guru and Kula priest from Puri Shreekshetra gave them landed property and established them in Dhenkanal. King Hari Singh Bidhyadhar was able to capture the hearts of his people and also established himself as a knowledgeable, pious, and kind hearted king. During his reign Dhenkanal was prosperous. The people lived happily without any fear.

After him, his son Lokanath Rai Singh Bhramarabara Rai took over the throne and ruled Dhenkanal from 1594 till 1615. Gajapati Maharaja conferred him with Rai Singh Bhramarabara Rai title because of their cordial relationship in the past and also during his reign. After King Lokanath Rai Singh Bhramarabara Rai was enthroned to expand his state territory he defeated the kings of Kolkola, Dalijoda, Darpan, Madhupur and included these states with Dhenkanal. He also included the area in between Brahamani and Ramiala River in Dhenkanal after his victory in the war. King Lokanath wasn't only a mighty king but also a popular king. During his reign, the people lead a peaceful life.

He also received special privileges during his Jagannath darshan at Puri by Gajapati Maharaja. Till how long he will go by the palanquin, how will the torch go, how will he be fanned, all these arrangements were made accordingly. Few people get this respect and because of this Dhenkanal royal family's devotion and royal excellence were propounded.

After him, his son Balabhadra Rai Singh Bhramarabara ruled from 1615 till 1641 and his son Nilambar Rai Singh Bhramarabara ruled from 1641 till 1680. During their reign Prjanga, Baniapada area was acquired and included in Dhenkanal. During their reign, there was an improvement in the agricultural sector so people lived happily and peacefully.

From 1680 till 1708 Nursingha Bhramarabara was enthroned as the king of Dhenkanal and he ruled. He also expanded his state territory. At present Kamakhya Nagar subdivision's Gada Nursingha Prasad, Gadangapur, Jenadesha, and Madhupur regions few areas were included in Dhenkanal after his victory in the war. King Hari Singh Bidyadhara started the construction of Balaram temple and the incomplete work was completed by King Nursingha Bhramarabara. Jauli Pokhari is one of his glories. Construction of Anekoteswar Mahadeb temple, land for

Lord Jagannath in Jamunakot village, in Khokasa, Blibo, Jakiya, Riya, Mathatentuli, Jaridamali , and Khuntajharida Mathas was established. It's his immortal glory. During his reign, many scholars, knowledgeable persons, saints, and the most powerful Baishnab guru were present in the king's court and discussed very frequently regarding religion and knowledge. The people lived happily in his good governance and the rituals of the god and goddesses were performed piously.

After King Nursingha Bhramarabara his son, Kunja Bihari ruled from 1708 till 1728. King Kunja Bihari was extremely pious. At many times he invited the saints and Baishnaba's to give a religious discourse. He was ensouled with Krishna devotion and wrote a book named 'Premasila 'based on the eternal love of Radha Krishna. He raised war against the king of Angul and captured few areas and included it in Dhenkanal. He used"Maa Ramchandi's" garland and sword in this war and was victorious so he set up a village named Khadga Prasad. He had lots of faith in "Maa Ramachandi" He was devoted towards god and looked after the management of the temples and mathas. As a king, he reigned with good governance and kept the people happy.

From the year 1728 till 1741 Dhenkanal was ruled by King Kunja Bihari's son Braja Bihari Rai Singh Bhramarabara. Braja Bihar's second brother Benudhar Harichandan Singh renounced the worldly pleasures and became a saint. It is said that the dutiful observance of the law in one's life enhances the family dharma. Prince Benudhar developed an aversion towards the royal family's richness, pleasure, and comfort and renounced all and decided to live like a saint and demonstrated the family's greatness.

During King Kunja Bihari's reign Mugulas, Pathanas and Barghi Marathas evaded the state, dishonestly took away the wealth, and very cruelly showed their tyranny. To protect the people from this tyranny King Kunja Bihari was always ready with his army and every time confronted his subjects. During his reign, the king of Angul was in war with him in the border of Angul's and occupied few areas and as a result, King Kunja Bihari fought back with bravery and brought back those areas again under his reign. He wasn't only satisfied with this. He raised wars and extended his territory to Budha Panka and kept the honor of the royal family. He defeated the king of Tigiriya and included few areas in Dhenkanal. King Kunja Bihari was a Bishnu devotee and he also composed few poems based on Bhakti rasa.

After King Kunja Bihari, his son Damodar Rai Singh Bhramarabara reigned only from 1741 till 1743. Kalakala state which was in the east of Dhenkanal had an embroilment with Dhenkanal, so King Damodar Rai Singh Bhramarabara defeated Kalakala state in the war. The King of Kalakala felt humiliated and as he didn't have enough soldiers to raise war so he took the help of the tyrannous plunderage. It wasn't possible for anyone to enter Dhenkanal as it was surrounded by forests and mountains. Other than that Dhenkanal's good governance, vast powerful trained army and the blessings of the god protected it. At that time, all over the country, there was abhorrence towards Mughals, Pathanas , and Barghi Marathas. People were scared of their tyranny, plunderage, and deceit. During that time the King of Kalakala invited Barghi Marathas and asked for their help. It wasn't only a disgraceful act of the king but also it reflected his inferiority complex and weak values. From this time Dhenkanal state Barghi's rage began.

King Damodar didn't have a son so after him Jagannath Bhramarabara began his reign. Jagannath Bhramarabara was King Damodar's uncle's son. He adorned the throne from a young age. King Jagannath Bhramarabara reigned only for a year. Among the two sons of Jagannath Bhramarabara, the elder one was physically handicapped and the younger one was a minor. During that time the Barghi Marathas were collecting illegal taxes from different states by force. They cruelly ransacked and burnt the houses. To collect the tax from Dhenkanal their oppression increased day by day. Therefore to protect the state from oppression and cruelty with the consent of all King Braja Bihari's third brother Ghanashyam's son Trilochan was made the king in the year 1745-46.

Till the year 1785 King Trilochan Mahendra Bahadur reigned the state. It was a time of pride and dignity; it will be always remembered in Dhenkanal's history. About his long reign, about the justice, truth, dharma, and bravery are written in the history which can never be forgotten. King Trilochana himself was a brave warrior. His war technique was very skillful. He very calmly and with intelligence always won the battle. In his vast army were literate, trained, and skillful warriors (Pikemen), warriors on elephant back(Elephantry), warriors on horses (Cavalry), Telenga and Naga warriors. Other than them were Paikas and Khandayata.

The battalion deployed for the protection of the state was always alert. It was their profession and along with that, they did agriculture. When they were called by the chieftain or when it was necessary under the guidance and instruction of their chieftain they fought with the enemies. The warriors and the Khandayatas have kept their tradition alive but because of the change in time, involvement of the self- centered people they are lifeless. They are now divided into many party and sub parties and have forgotten the power of unionism. Khandayata who represent supreme power of warfare have lost its originality and is living in a parochial society of illiteracy, superstitions, and have lost their true identity.

King Trilochana gradually increased his territory as he defeated the kings of Athagarh, Tigiria, Hindol, Palahada, and Keojhara. As a result, the defeated kings to take revenge seek the help of Marathas. Before that during the reign of Jagannath Bhramarabara cruelty and plunderage were already attempted by the Barghi Marathas. The Barghi Marathas tried their best to impose a full tax on Dhenkanal but King Trilochana condemned their act of cruelty and plunderage and showed them his might. Their oppression stopped because of this. King Trilochan very candidly denied giving the tax because Dhenkanal wasn't a state which was won by the Marathas.

As a free state, it wasn't necessary to give the Maratha rulers the tax. It wasn't possible for King Trilochan to carry out the verbal order of the Marathas to give them the tax as he never wanted to downcast the bravery of his soldiers or himself. He could never unveil the helplessness of his prosperous state in front of the cruel oppressors. It was unrealistic, impossible, and against his self-respect. A respectable crowned king of a free state and with a lot of faith in the strength of his soldiers, King Trilochan very wisely thought and firmly decided that he will raise war against the defeated kings and the Barghi Marathas. As he constantly opposed and didn't give the tax to the Marathas, once in the year 1779 and again in the year 1781 to bring Dhenkanal under them and to take revenge the soldiers of Maratha reign fought the war near Motari and Sathiyae Bati.

The Maratha army fought for 18 days and was finally defeated. The ego of the great army of Maratha was shattered in front of Dhenkanal's unconquerable power. The famous poet of that time, Brajanath Badajena wrote "Samar Tarang" which depicts the true story and the details of the war and gave it a historic significance by using high standard language in his poetry. Dhenkanal's immortal poet Brajanath Badajena is a symbol of pride for Odiya literature, and his birthplace Kabera has done its duty diligently by giving a vivid description of the war at Sathiyae Bati. This is accepted in literature and history.

The Britishers were applying their diplomatic strategy and were capturing the areas one by one. The powers of Marathas and others were slowly diminishing because of their unrighteousness and they didn't expect defeat from the internal strong states. They were always making strategies to defeat these undefeatable strong states. The Maratha rulers took the help of the Britishers who were slowly becoming powerful as they had the modern warfare technique and tried to hide their real intention of hoodwinking to defeat the independent and brave kings like the king of Dhenkanal and other states.

The Britishers took the advantage of this by helping the country's oppressive group by rendering little help. In that way, it can be said that the war which was fought in Dhenkanal was a part of the Independence movement. The rulers of this country who took the help of the Britishers to achieve their goal couldn't realize the consequence of asking for help from them at that time. They couldn't foresee the future as they didn't have the capacity of perception. At that time Gajapati Maharaja, few administrators like the king of Dhenkanal and other states who had a love for their country, those who visualized an independent India, those who didn't become the slaves of others for their personal benefits stood firmly against the oppressor and deceitful and suppressed them. They are given the right place in history.

King Trilochan has made a place in the pages of history after the 18 days battle. It was also told that it was a battle of righteousness against injustice. It was a battle to suppress the cruel oppressors, a battle against the decisive Britishers, and a battle to keep self-respect and humanity alive.

From the year 1745 till 1785 was eventful according to the situation. According to the proposal of the Marathas, there was a peace treaty between the two sides and there was an end to the war. The Marathas to show their respect towards King Trilochan and to acknowledge his power conferred him with "Mahendra Bahadur" title. Gajapati Maharaja approved this. After King Trilochan his son Dayanidhi Mahendra Bahadur began his reign from 1785 till 1795 in Dhenkanal. He wasn't inclined towards expanding his territory by war. He continued his reign and focused on the happiness and peace of his subjects. King Dayanidhi didn't have any children.

After his death, his brother's son Mansingh took the charge of the reign and continued for a year from 1795 till 1796. As King Mansingh didn't have a son so after him Trilochan Mahendra Bahadur's one of the sons of Ramachandra Singh Mahendra Bahadur took over the royal throne from the year 1796 till 1807 and ruled Dhenkanal. He didn't have the lust of expanding his state. He focused on the internal issues of the state. He was spiritual and did his administrative work in a disciplined way. During King Ramachandra's reign, Balaram temple's wall was made. By this time, the Britishers had already started ruling over India and had occupied many parts of India. But Kalinga or Utkala was still not included in their reign.

King Ramachandra didn't have a son. After him, King Krushnachandra Mahendra Bahadur took over the royal throne and began his reign from the year 1807 till 1822.King Krushnachandra was a mighty king but he didn't pay attention towards expanding his territory rather he paid attention for the protection of Dhenkanal's border. He constructed a reservoir in his state and visited the pilgrimage like Shrrekshetra Puri, Jajapur, and many other pilgrimages in northern India. He led a spiritual life. His lifestyle influenced the people of Dhenkanal as a result the people of Dhenkanal were inclined towards spirituality and had faith in it.

King Krushnachandra didn't have a child that's why after him King Trilochan Singh Mahendra Bahadur's cousin King Jagannath Bhramarabara's grandson Shyamsundar Mahendra Bahadur took over the throne and began his reign from 1822 till 1830. King Shyamsundar was a brave warrior. During this time the war was fought between him and the king of Angul near Budha Panka. He defeated the king of Angul and the territory of Dhenkanal was expanded till Budha Panka. Other than this King Shyamsundar also included Badamba state's Jhumudia and Klika Prasad these two villages in Dhenkanal.

With this battle, the expansion of the Dhenkanal state stopped. By that time India was ruled by the British rulers. The kings of Angul, Talcher, Badmba, Tigria, and other nearby states were envious of King Shyamsundar's bravery and became revengeful. They spoke ill and brought baseless charges against him and put it in front of the Gadjat Mahaliya. But virtuous and popular King Shyamsundar wasn't affected by this. He was respected as the king who won many battles.

King Shyamsundra Mahendra Bahadur was childless. His adopted son who was a minor, King Bhagiratha Mahendra Bahadur took over the throne in the year 1830 but on his behalf, the administrative work was looked after by his mother and other employees of the royal court. He took over the administrative work from the year 1842 and continued till the year 1877. King Bhagirathi had good governance; he was lawful, disciplined, religious, knowledgeable, and spiritual. Whenever King Bhagiratha began a new work or thought of doing any work he always kept in mind that it follows the approved laws and rules mentioned in Gita, Bhagabat, Ramayana, and other scriptures. After this was confirmed by him, he went ahead with his work.

He never did any work against ethics. His spiritual life was reflected in such a way that, any injustice or deceitful activities couldn't touch him. He motivated and advised the employees of the royal court to follow the path of righteousness, to be benevolent, and to do render their service to others. Because of his motivational and idealistic approach, the employees of the royal court and the people had respect for him. It was more prestigious, significant and noble than the royal honor.

During his tenure, he did the land settlement in Dhenkanal. As a result, the king and the people could get an account of their landed property and were sure about its existence. According to that tax was also calculated keeping the comfort of all in mind. King Bhagiratha gave the permission to clean the forest and convert it into agricultural land. He paid attention to agriculture, education, and health protection. He established many upper primary schools and established a minor school near his fort. As he was a knowledgeable king so he appointed many scholars, poets, and writers in his court and discussed with them regarding shastra and royal administration.

He established a Sanskrit college in his name. He constructed the Jaulin Pokhari Matha and adjacent to it Nursingh Sagar pond and for its maintenance gave tax- free land. The deaf and dumb, saints and guests when visited Dhenkanal they used the matha and were fed with purely vegetarian food. He also constructed an artistically designed Jagmohana , a cookhouse and water pavilion in Kapilash. At Deogao Balaram temple's mukhasala, Paschimaswar temple's mukhasala, the wall of his own fort Balaram temple and Jaganmohana, Shankarpur, Bhapur, Baulapur roads, etc were few of his glory. He also did many developmental works for the simple, innocent, and illiterate tribal.

During his reign, he ordered to do all the court proceedings in Odiya language and also showed interest in executing the same. During the time of need, he gave the food grains to people from his warehouse and for that, he never kept any terms and conditions. The people returned the quantity of grain borrowed after a good harvest. Because of this people didn't fall into the trap of the landlords and could make arrangements for their needs during requirement. During the famine, King Bhagirtha Pratap Mahendra Bahadur, not only to the people of Dhenkanal but also to all the famine- affected people of Odisha, gave money, grains from his warehouse and saved their life. He gained a lot of name and fame because of this. During any type of natural calamities, King Bhagiratha helped the people. Because of his great virtues, for his administrative skills in which he gave importance to humanity, he was conferred with Maharaja Title.

To establish the first printing press in Odisha King Bhagirtha rendered financial support to Trading Company. For the expansion of education and to compose educative books on Higher English he gave a lot of money. To create a competitive spirit among the students he also made arrangements for financial help. To keep the dignity of Odiya language intact and for the rapid improvement of the language, the steps that he took were an epoch and an example that was set for others to follow.

In order to feed milk every day to Mahima cult's founder Mahima Gosaein, Maharaja Bhagirtha Mahendra Bahadur made arrangements and allocated landed property at Mahima Pitha ,Joranda . At times, The British Commissioner of those days solicited his help and forwarded many difficult and legal problems for its solution to the Maharaja.

Maharaja Bhagirtha kept in mind the complete faith of others in him and did the judgment judiciously. Maharaja Bhagiratha was issueless. At the time of his death, adopted son, King Dinabandhu Mahendra Bahadur was a minor so in his name, the state administration was carried out.

From the year 1877 on behalf of the minor king Dinabandhu Mahendra Pratap, Banamali Singh was appointed to carry out the arrangements made by the British government state of order and he continued with the administrative work. Shri Fakir Mohan Senapati who was one of the renowned writers of Odiya literature was appointed as associate controller of the state administration. During his stay at Dhenkanal, Fakir Mohan translated Hindi Ramayana into Odiya.

King Dinabandhu Mahendra Bahadur ruled till the year 1885. He was benevolent, compassionate, considerate, and god fearing person. He began the education and health related developmental activities in the state. He also did much developmental work in Kapilash. His wife, Banai king's daughter Annapurna was in the true sense"Maa Annapurna". Sculpturing the Narayana idol at Kapilash and to consecrate it is the culmination of swadharma which gained him immense name and fame.

After the demise of King Dinabandhu, his son Rajashree Shura Pratap ruled from the year 1885 till 1918. He was hardly 5 to 6 months old during his father's demise so according to the Court of Ward an authority was appointed to continue with the administrative work.

In person, he took care of the administrative work from the year 1907 and has done many great works. During the reign of Rajshree Shura Pratap, many temples were constructed and the developmental work of those was done. The beginning of Ratha Yatra, construction of roads, water reservoirs, the betterment of villages through Grama Sabha, development in the cultural aspect, literary meetings, help during the famine and other natural calamities, etc are an example of his saintly efficacy which is revealed every time and everywhere. He died at the early age of 34 in the year 1918.

After King Sura Pratap's demise his son Shankar Pratap was enthroned in the year 1918. At that time Shankar Pratap was a minor as he was only 14 years old. So till he became a major Dhenkanal was ruled directly by the British according to the British Court of Ward. Late Rajkishore Tripathy was appointed as Dewan. After King Shankar Pratap became a major in the year 1925 till the integration of the princely states he ruled till the year 1947.

Dhenkanal's dynasty was founded in the year 1530 with only a small amount of land of Karamula Patana. At that time because of knowledge, power, art, skills, and capability, the kings of his dynasty expanded their territory far and wide. The Dhenkanal state is today's Kamakhya Nagar, and Dhenkanal Sadar Subdivision in total. In the mountainous region with the difficulty in the transportation, with the old techniques of warfare training the soldiers, disciplined administrative work, forbearance, justice and to establish a trustworthy relationship and belongingness between the king and his subjects was possible for the exceptional kings of the dynasty.

They not only expanded Dhenkanal state by war but also bestowed their love and affection and worked for the development of people of the occupied areas. Being inspired by the king's fame, the conscientious Khandayata Paika soldiers gave their best and set an example of their skills. The kings of this dynasty were always inspired by virtue, knowledge, intellect, and leadership. They were devoted to their motherland and always strived hard to protect it and to retain its dignity. There was a sense of belongingness, faith, interpersonal relationship, understanding, and respect between the king and his subjects.

It was only because of these reasons the kings of Dhenkanal were blessed and got the support of their subjects and could expand their state. As a symbol of benevolence, spirituality, knowledge, secularism, and bravery the kings of this dynasty had made their names in history. Many learned and knowledgeable people of Odisha and from other places have recorded the glory of this dynasty in their books and in history. Magazines like Utkala Deepika, Mukura ,Samar Taranga, Madhupur Koili, Balabhadra Boli, Rasa Binoda, Budaranka like books , the presently published books and magazines and Cobden Ramsay's "Feudatory States of Orissa ",Sir John Beans "Memories of Bengal Civilians" "Princes of India" publication and Rosita Forbes's " India of Princes" are many true stories. These illustrious appreciative stories of Dhenkanal are a burning lamp that has illuminated the glory of the dynasty and has made it immortal. There is no doubt about it.

The royal family of Dhenkanal never blew its own trumpet. The kings of this dynasty realized and understood that while performing noble deeds like donation and showing benevolence if a person feels proud and try to propagate his noble deeds it lessens. Their noble deeds found a place in many magazines, books and history with fond pursuit. There is enough evidence of this in the books written by the writers of that time.

The contemporary writers also have written about the bright persona, immaculate personality, and benevolence of the kings of this dynasty. In the autobiography written by Justice Radhakishore, an autobiography by Rajkishore Ram, Kalandi Charan Panigrahi's written autobiography, Justice Harihara Mahapatra's autobiography there are many true and significant stories about the politics and the political leaders. In contrary to these write- ups, when today's tribune's activity and administrative policy along with that of general public's political, social, and financial state is pursued; the false vouch for nationality is examined thoroughly and is justly scrutinized then the acceptable and unacceptable is clearly distinguishable for common man.

Few people try to hide the truth and take the path of falsehood, injustice, immorality, and corruption. They do many dreadful works with their pretension and cleverness to establish them in society for a short time. But truth can never be hidden and it slowly finds its way from the darkness to revelation. Finally, these pretentious entities are unmasked but still, they don't mend their ways and search for another disguise. Their pretentious demeanour is the reason for the downfall of society.

The kings of this dynasty were associated with the country's patriots like Subhash Chandra Bose, his father Janakinath Bose, and his family members. The warrant was issued as King Shankar Pratap, my fourth brother Tiki Bhai, Prince Gourandra Pratap Singh Deo, and I helped Netaji Subhash Chandra Bose to escape. But as the king of Dhenkanal was 'A' class administrator to arrest him wasn't easy. Because of this we went through lots of harassment and mental agony and had to leave the palace.

Till the warrant was there against us ,from the year 1944 till 1946 we spent a nomadic life and also lead a refugee life under the canopy of the kings of Balangir, Sareikela, Boudh, Calcutta, Patiala, Ooty, Travencore, Panchkot,and some kings of other countries like Shinghal, Lahore and Rawalpindi. At this moment of distress and uncertainty, King Shankar Pratap's patience and daring nature's vivid description is written in the book "Story of the Integration of Indian States" by V.P Menon, Sardar K.M Panikar , Pundit H.N Kunjru, and Dr.B.C Roy's opinion is mentioned and Charles Chenevix Trench's " Viceroy's Agent" named book throw light on this. Few extracts from "Viceroy's Agents" are included in Annexure IV.

POST SCRIPT- Baji Rout
9,Vidyut Marg, Bhubaneswar
Date: 25.04.1997

A few days back a meeting was arranged in memory of Baji Rout. In that meeting, many notable people spoke about Baji Rout and about Dhenkanal's administration. In the year 1938, the Praja Mandal Agitation movement was seen in many princely states. In Dhenkanal's Bhuban area Praja Mandal agitators gave many sentimental speeches. People became agitated and it became difficult to control them.

British government brought the troop from Punjab and other states and integrated with the troops of Kharsawan, Sareikela, Dhenkanal, and Khairagad and made Eastern State Agency Joint Police and suppressed the Praja Mandal Agitation but people didn't step back. One day when the people got biased by listening to Praja Mandal activists and became violent, to create fear among them firing was ordered. Despite of those agitators didn't give up. At that Gadjat police weren't given arms and ammunitions. They were only provided with limited arms and ammunition for Blank firing purposes.

Baji Rout certainly died in the firing, In the firing six to seven of them were also injured- this is also true but in this incident because of whose firing Baji Rout died can't be said. They blamed my husband Shankar Pratap whereas Bhuban is 15 miles away from Dhenkanal palace. We heard that the police troop was trying to cross the river in a boat to go to Bhuban, at that time the boatmen left the boat and ran away. Dhenkanal's troop cut the anchor rope with their riffles Bayonet, rowed the boat from Bhuban to the other side. Baji Rout died from whose firing can't be said correctly.

After Baji Rout's death his dead body was taken out in a procession at Cuttack by my Co- father- in- law- the king of Kalahandi Pratap Keshari Deo who was the former MP and was a student in Ravensahaw College Cuttack at that time. When I read about Baji Rout and his story in "Samaj" ,in the first column it was written :

Shirdi Sai Baba has told one of his disciples –The disciple was telling about a person to Sai Baba who wasn't present there. Baba said,"A person who tries to defame others is like a pig who tastes his faeces and feels happy. It is something similar to that".

We are born as human beings because of many good deeds in the past life. Instead of praying to God, we indulge ourselves in criticizing others, plotting against others and show our ego which isn't praiseworthy.

In the year 1957, I was a contestant from Kamakhya Nagar constituency for Vidhan Sabha and Shri Surendra Mohanty was a contestant for parliament. Many times I have crossed the river near Bhuban. I also went to Baji Rout's mother's house. His mother never uttered a single word against the king's administration rather she gave me a lot of respect. When I was campaigning for the vote and was going from one village to another village; was meeting the people of Dhenkanal to know about their well-being- at that time King Shankar Pratap Mahendra Bahadur and my mother-in-law Priya Devi accompanied me. I can never forget their benevolent nature. I bow down my head in front of them as a mark of respect.

(Quoting from Radhanath Grathabali)
Eechanti dambike haste rakhibaku samasthan ka bhagya dori

Matra nija bhagya kala hastae aeha pakanti hele pasori
Shakti nahi batsa kahari jagatae niyatiki naba nija eecha matae!

My second brother-in-law Shri Shriesha Pratap Singh Deo and the fourth brother-in-law Shri Gourendra Pratap Singh Deo translated Sambhu Khestra Kapilash and Badajena's Samar Tarang and received Sahitya Academy Award. Because of ill fate- my second brother-in-law Shri Shriesha Pratap Singh Deo has left for heavenly abode. Shri Gourendra Pratap Singh Deo and the younger brother Shri Samarendra Pratap Singh Deo are still alive. I pray for their long life.

With the blessings of Lord Jagannath I conclude my writing.

Ratna Prava Devi

POST SCRIPT-2 (My Family Life)
9,Vidyut Marg, Bhubaneswar
Date: 25.04.1997

I am mentioning some of the stories of my life. My marriage was solemnized with King Shankar Pratap Mahindra Bahadur of Dhenkanal. Though I was his maternal uncle's daughter but priests had positively concurred to our marriage by following *'maternal uncle's daughter of south'* rule. Though years of conjugal life had passed with happiness and bliss, for a long time, I couldn't bear a child. After visiting Mother Kamakhyaa's place; completing worships and rituals as suggested by priests there, finally we were blessed with Kamakhyaa Prasad as our son and our life was filled with more happiness and bliss.

My mother in law was a very religious person. She lived the life of a saint after death of my father in law. She had immense devotion in prayers, gods and goddesses. My esteemed father in law Rajarshee Sura Pratap Mahindra Bahadur had built Soura Krishnadham mansions on both of their names at Sri Kunjakant. She used to draw some solace by daily worshipping Radhakrishna along with eight sakhis. She had published a book 'Bhakti Puspanjali" for small children. The book was published using melody and rhythm (swara-lipi) so that small children can easily understand them. She had written a book in Bengali titled "Bhakti Katha" (Devotional Stories). She has many writings on prayers to Sri Kunjakant and other gods. She had also written many books including a book on 'how to play harmonium'.

My second son is Pattayata Matru Prasad Singh Deo (King's second son is called Pattayat). We had also named him after goddess. He is also very religious. He loves to read religious scriptures like Gita, Mahabharat and Ramayan. He has collected many religious books. He enjoys gaining knowledge by reading Hindi, Odiya and English newspapers every day. He enjoys treating his brothers, relatives and guests. He had common health issues on his ear and throat as during childhood days as he suffered from German measles and Para Typhoid. We had taken him to Europe for treatment. We had done testing of his ear and throat at Manchester Deaf and Dumb School in England. After showing him to doctors in Switzerland, he was administered lonesion. Sometimes, we feel sad for him but never neglected on our duty for him. He was given home schooling by keeping a teacher at home. Being very intelligent, he had learnt how to bind books from his father. He had cured many people by preparing herbal medicines. He finishes any work assigned to him with greater precision. May god bless him with long life- that's my prayer to lord Jagannath.

I had five brother-in-laws. All of them have given due respect to me as their elder sister in law. The youngest ones- Tiki and Saana were always with me. As I was barren for long years, many a times, I used to forget the pain of being issueless due to their presence around me. My husband Raja Sahib also treated them like sons and always gave attention to their wellbeing. Today most of them have left for heavenly abode. Only Gourendra Pratap and Samarendra Pratap are around. I am praying to God for their well-being. Let them live happy and healthier. My co-sisters were also like my sisters. Only two are surviving from five of them.

My family life has passed through all bliss. All those who are alive now, let our survival be guided by the refuse at god's pious feet- that's my internal wish.

(Ratna Prava Devi)

Annexure-I

Constitution of Council

As his highness king of Dhenkanal is thinking about setting up a council and is also a requisite, this order is being issued that the council will function as per following:
- High Highness king Of Dhenkanal
  President
- Pattayat N P Singh Deo, B.A.
  Assistant President
- Diwan Bahadur D N Das, B.A.
  Judicial Member
- Prince S P Singhdeo, B L.   Home Member
- Following subjects will be discussed in the council and final decisions will be made
- All matters related to rules and processes; nature and application of rules and orders related to any department of governance
- Appointment of employees for higher class jobs
- Laying off or removal of all employees engaged in higher posts in any departments of the state
- All matters related to practice or withdrawal of rules under different laws or part thereof, for the state
- All matters and events related to land settlement,

renewal, irrigation and their general rules
- All matters related to general rules and procedures related budget and financial matters
- All materials related to foreign affairs (extradition). If his highness king of Dhenkanal, on his own, is considering some issues without the advice of the council can also act so.
- All matters, under the jurisdiction of the individual member or members can discuss them in the executive council if they consider the matter worth being discussed.
- Distribution of portfolios
- Any special/specific matter that His Highness king of Dhenkanal orders for discussion and decision.
- The final decision will be taken in the council by majority. Opinion of the president shall not be considered. But the final decision of the council will be dependent on his final approval or special judicial powers
- His highness of Dhenkanal will have all the powers to govern and supervise over the matters under the ageis of assistant president and other council members.
- The executive council meeting will be called for on the direct order of the president or from headquarters during his absence; on the matters of emergency or special event; by the direct orders of assistant president along with the signature of the secretary or through advertising.
- All the minutes of meeting will be recorded in minute's book or information booklet. The book will be signed by the president and remain with the secretary.
- This order of His highness kind of Dhenkanal will be

applicable from 1st April 1936 untill further orders.
- The detailed list of subjects under the control of executive council
- Following shall be under the administration of assistant president
- Political, foreign and employment department
- Finance
- State Secretariat
- Treasury, land audit and all other revenue matters including taxes
- Revenue department like certificate, mutation patta etc
- Forest
- Research work
- General supervision
- Administration of home member
- Development department
- Education
- Medical and health
- Police and excise
- Ideal agriculture temple and parks
- Stores department
- Jail and printing press
- Rural development work
- Agriculture
- Fisheries
- Business and commerce
- Local self-government
- State granary
- Mines
- PWD and irrigation department
- Administration under judicial member
- Law and justice

- Nazraati (office of the Nazir)
- The record room (mahafiz khaana)
- State gazette

With permission from
N.P Singh Deo
(Prime Minister)

Constitution of High Court

Whereas the ruler considers it expedient and desirable that the State of Dhenkanal should have a High Court of Justice, it is hereby ordered as follows:

1. There shall be a high course named as "The High court of Judicature at Dhenkanal" exercising the extra ordinary original Jurisdiction and appellate and revisional jurisdiction, both Civil and Criminal as provided respectively in the Code of Civil Procedure and in the Code of Criminal Procedure now in force within the territorial limits of the state.

2. The High Court shall consist of a Chief Judge and as many judges not exceeding 3 as the Ruler may from time to time think fit to appoint, who shall be selected from among the persons qualified as hereinafter mentioned Viz.
   A barrister or an Advocate of not less than 10 years standing or
   A person who has held judicial office not inferior to that of a subordinate judge or a District Officer or a Judge of Small Cause court either in British India or any Indian State for not less than five years.

3. The high court shall ordinarily exercise its appellate and revisional powers by a bench of two judges of that Court
   (b) The jurisdiction of the high court may be exercised

by a single judge of that court in the following matters only and until further orders in no others

i) On the Criminal side: granting bails, admitting appeals and admitting and disposing of petitions for revision of orders of the sessions judge and magistrates

ii) On the Civil Side: disposing second appeals of the cases in suits valued at not more than Rs 200/ and revision of civil matters.

iii) The Chief Judge may hear any civil suit in exercise of the original jurisdiction of the High Court as the Ruler may be pleased to direct

4   (a) The High Court may make rules for the constitution of a full bench of the court and may by such rules prescribe the mode of determining which judges shall constitute as a Full Bench when such sittings becomes necessary (b) The Chief Judge will determine the constitution of the Bench and distribution of cases

5   The Chief Judge may transfer any case from the file of any judge sitting alone to the file of any other judge or bench of the court.

6   Any judge of the High court sitting alone and any bench of judges thereof not being a full bench may refer, for the decision of the bench of two judges or of a full bench, any question of law or custom having the force of law or of the construction of any document or of the admissibility of any evidence, arising in any case before the Judge or the Bench and such judge or bench shall dispose of the case in accordance with the decision of the Bench to which the question has been referred.

7   (a) Where there is difference of opinion among the judges composing any bench of the High Court, the

decision shall be in accordance with the decision of the majority of those judges (b) If there is such a majority (i) the decision shall be in accordance with the opinion of the senior judge of the bench (ii)In other cases, the bench before which the difference has arisen shall refer the point or points of difference to such other judges of the court as may be selected by the Chief Judge and the case shall be disposed of in accordance with the decision of such judge.

8   The High Court may from Time to Time by notification make rules not inconsistent with any regulation or order for the time being in force (a) declaring what personal shall be permitted to practice as pleaders in the High Court and other courts subordinate there to (b) declaring what person shall be permitted to practice as petition writers in the subordinate courts of the state, regulating the conduct of business by persons so practicing, determining the authority by which breach of rules under this clause shall be dealt with and prescribing the procedure to be followed by such authority (c) providing for the translation, if any of any papers filed or produced in the High Court and requiring payment of the expenses incurred therefor (d) prescribing the persons who shall be entitled to inspect records of any court regulating the procedure for the inspection of such records of any court, or for obtaining a copy of the same and prescribing the fees payable for such inspections and for copies (e) prescribing the travelling and other expenses to be allowed to witness in civil cases and the fees to be allowed to Commissioners appointed by the civil courts (f) prescribing costumes to be worn in court by the

judges of the High Court and the courts subordinate thereto and by legal practitioners (g) conferring and imposing on the Ministerial Officers of the High Court and of the courts subordinate thereto such powers and duties of a non-judicial or quasi-judicial nature as it thinks fit and regulating the mode in which powers and duties so conferred and imposed shall be exercised and performed (h) prescribing forms and registers to be used in the subordinate courts (i) providing for the inspection of the subordinate courts and the supervision of the working thereof and (j) regulating all such matters as it may think fit with a view to promoting the efficiency of the judicial and ministerial officers of the courts of the state and maintaining proper discipline among such officers

9   The High Court shall keep such registers, books and accounts as may be necessary for the transactions of the business of the court.

By order of the Ruler

Sd/
N P Singh Deo
Prime Minister

Abolition of Bethi (Slavery) System

Whereas it is considered expedient that Bethi System which is in vogue since time immemorial and has outlived its utility and is no longer suited to the temperament and outlook of the people in general and whereas the origin of the system is based on the fact that some reduction in the rental was allowed as an exchange of Bethi labor and whereas it is considered necessary to provide certain restrictions to meet emergency:- it is hereby ordered that

(I) the bethi (Slavery) system will be abolished with effect from 1st April 1936 subject to the following reservations

    a) Social ceremony of the Ruling Family
    b) Shikar(Hunting)
    c) Forest Fire

In case of Kheda operations labor will have to be secured compulsorily of course on payment of wages rates of which will be determined on such occasions. Rates of wages for labor to be required for works of other departments of the state will also have to be determined in view of prevailing economic conditions from time to time.

(II) In lieu of Forced labor the tenants concerned will contribute Rs0.40 per rupee to the state fund in view of the fact that the state should be compensated for the loss of such labor.

(III) That all Lakhrajadars barring Debottar and Khanja Lakhrajdar, other rent free Jagirdars and their stitiban tenants will contribute at the same rate calculated over the rentals at which their holdings would have been assessed upon as ordinary tenants of the state as the benefits they would derive from the abolition of the system will be undeniable and considerable.

By the Order of the Ruler

Sd/
N P Singh Deo
Prime Minister

Annexure-2
Court(Darbar)'s Address Dhenkanal
DHENKANAL
STATE GAZETTE
Extra Ordinary

PUBLISHED BY AUTHORITY
Dhenkanal 26th June 1939

CONSTITUTION OF THE COUNCIL
26.6.1939
DHENKANAL

The State of Dhenkanal may justly feel proud of its administration which from the time of its illustrious founder Sri Hari Singh in 1529 AD up to the present has always been run with the sole objective of promoting the cultural, social and economic welfare of the people and in this respect Dhenkanal occupies perhaps a unique position among the states of Orissa, We use no language of convention when we say that no other state in Orissa can point to a record of more beneficial administration, broad based on the goodwill of grateful people/ We confidently assert that in the race for progress the people of this state have never fallen behind their brethren in any other state.

A resume of the progress achieved in the past during the time of each successive ruler will make this address inordinately long and we would briefly touch on some of the important features of the administration as recorded by eminent authorities. The great historian Mr W W Hunter who visited Dhenkanal in 1870 spoke of Dhenkanal as 'the most civilized of the tributary states though Mayurbhanj or the Peacock country was the largest' and of the rules as 'representing the very highest point of culture, moderation and justice, which any of the chiefs attained under the British.

The homage to grateful people must go back to that illustrious prince Maharaja Bhagirath Mahindra Bahadur who made extensive rent free grants to maintain the position and culture of the Brahmin community. He was one of the few worthies from whom emanated the initiatives to which the Ravenshaw college, The Temple Medical Hospital and The Cuttack Printing Press owed their origin. But for his charities, the progress of education in Orissa would have been put back by 50 years. Mr Stirling in his account of Orissa remarked 'The large percentage of the Brahmin population compared with the other Garjat states is accounted for by the fact that the previous chiefs of Dhenkanal and more particularly Maharaja Bhagirath Mahindra Bahadur an enlightened ruler and lover of Sanskrit literature made extensive grants of Lakhraj lands to learned brahmins and induced them to settle down in the state with a view to raise the standard of public morality.

This state can also boast of High English School established over 40 years ago when a similar institution could be found only in the State of Mayurbhanj and a Sanskrit tol – the only institution of its kind at the time of the establishment used to attract students from faraway places. Even now it occupies foremost place as a seat of Sanskrit learning. The expenditure of the state under the head of education has always been high. The amount generally spent under this head is nearly 13% of the total revenue. The percentage of literacy in this state is much higher when compared with that in neighboring states and British Districts.

With regard to the social advancement of the people this state can take claim the credit of effecting an improvement of a far reaching character. Up to the time of Maharaja Bhagirath Mahindra Bahadur, the aboriginal tribes used to go naked under a superstitious belief that the wearer of the cloth would fall victim to tigers. It was the personal influence of that noble ruler Maharaja Bhagirath Mahindra Bahadur which disabused the people of this erroneous impression and the people were for the first time induced to wear clothes and all the apparels were distributed free by that magnanimous Maharaja Bhagirath Mahindra Bahadur. For the stabilization of the society the efficient ruler of the state have bestowed free jagirs (rent free land) on the barbers, potters, blacksmiths, carpenters, washer man and men of different calling whose services were essential to the development of the society.

No less important were the efforts of the rulers of the state towards the spiritual advancement of people. A spirit of toleration has always marked the attitude of the Rulers towards the religious beliefs of the different sects of the Hindu community and the followers of other religions. The bulk of people are followers of Vaishnab cult and establishment of large number of shrines in different parts of the state point to the earnestness of the rulers to satisfy the religious carvings of the people. Even in recent times, Vaishnab preachers of high repute were brought to the holyland of ours which was sanctified by the visits of the great profounder of Vaishnab cult- Mahapravu Sri Chaitanya Deb and Mahima Goswami- the preacher of the Mahima cult. Every village in the state has a Bhagabat ghar (house).

The economic development of the people has always engaged the careful attention of the rulers of the state. The tenants have always had free access to the Rulers and a direct relationship subsist between the ruler and the tiller of the soil except in a few rent free tenures, but the percentage of such tenures is insignificant. Stable rights on the land were conferred in the state on people long before similar privileges were granted in other states. The security of the tenancy right induced the people to apply themselves whole heartedly to the improvement of their agricultural condition and they had advanced to comfort and prosperity to such a degree that as early as in 1818, Lt. Lawrence while passing through this state made the following remark

"The Mahal (palace) seems to have been one of natures favored spots, a sort of Peru on a small scale.' We may incidentally mention here that the incidence of taxation per head in the state is only Rs. 1.50 which is much less than what one gets in nearby states. The question of health and sanitation, the improvement of cattle and water supply in the state hav always occupies a prominent place in the consideration of the authorities. There are about 2000 tanks with the ambit of the state and to help the irrigation of important crops a big water reservoir was constructed in 1935, capable of irrigating about 2000 acres of land.

The reservation of sufficient gazing land in each village known as gochar marks a distinct step towards improvement of bovine population. A satisfactory increase in the number of hospitals and arrangements for combating outbreaks of epidemic diseases even in the outlying parts of the state constitute a marked feature of the administration.

The security of life and property is ensured by an efficient organization of the police. All laws of the state are codified and they are administered by impartial judiciary and the individual liberty of the people is never encroached upon The execution of such beneficial measures for a long and uninterrupted period in the various branches of administration resulted in a marked improvement in the social, cultural and economic development of the people and the high standard of administration obtaining in the state elicited the eloquent approbation of one of the eminent political officers of the Eastern State Agency Colonel Meek, C.M.G- the agent to the Governor General who was pleased to observe as follows:

"From what I have been able to see of the administration of your state, I have formed the opinion that it is a good administration and that your state takes a high place among the well administered states of this agency. I may tell- you stand well among the states of India generally in the matter of their governance'.

If we have alluded in some details to the past history of the state and the measures taken from time to time to improve the machinery of the administration and to the rights and privileges granted to them periodically, we have done so, with the intention of explaining to the people the solicitude that was bestowed in the past to secure the real progress of the subjects and the path we have steadfastly been following with a view to secure the same end.

On return from our Europe tour, in 1936 we realized the necessity of keeping pace with the new times and were glad to introduce several measures of reform for the better administration of the state. The most important of this was the establishment of a High court to inspire the confidence of the people in the administration of justice. Inauguration of an executive council marked another step of development of administrative machinery. Equally important was the announcement regarding the abolition of bethi system of compulsory labor which had outgrown its usefulness.

Encourage by the success of these reforms, we have now decided to go further and ti introduce for the first time an elective element in the administration for the civic welfare of the people. We have an abiding faith in the loyal cooperation of our subjects and if there were some indications in the recent past of disaffection in a section of the people, it was due to the extraneous influences. We believe the effect of those baneful influences is by this time over and the traditional loyalty or our beloved people will reassert itself. However, to ensure an atmosphere of goodwill and cooperation, we shall by proclaiming remission of six months to all persons undergoing imprisonment in the hails of the state. This will have the effect of procuring immediate release of 56 prisoners in the sadar jail of whom 43 persons were undergoing jail for offences in connection with the unrest leaving only 14 persons under this head in the jail whose cases will be considered in the due course. The same applies to the case of prisoners in Murhi Jail. We also direct the withdrawal of proceedings against all persons awaiting trial under section 17 of the Criminal Law Amendment Act.

A believe in constitutional process must look back to his country's golden days wherein lies the seed of his country's future advancement. The village pancahyat system is indigenous to India and it really represents the earliest democratic institutions in the world. The edifice of local self-government must be built upon the basis of these village panhayats. Moved by an earnest desire to see our people rapidly advance along the path of constitutional progress, we have decided to resuscitate the old village panchayat. The idea is to have ine independent panchayat in each big village and to group of smaller ones into various panchayat units. Village panchayats as you know are the foundation stone in any scheme and structure of Local Self Government and we hope they will prove the means of arousing a greater interest in the people for self-government as well as infuse in them a spirit of responsibilities and a sense of proper civic duty, and teach them to subordinate interest of the individual to the larger and higher interest of the community.

These panchayats will be constituted on purely elective basis of adult franchisee with nominated sripanchas. They will be vested with the administration, primary education as local educational authority and will further be given the privileges of performing a number of useful and indispensable duties for themselves such as the organization of measures for the improvement of health, sanitation, irrigation, water supply and agriculture. This we trust will bring people into closer contact with the administrative authorities of our state and through them keep up in direct touch with every day progress. These measures will further afford great opportunities to our people to train themselves in the art of administration that will ultimately bring about the material development of our state.

We entertain higher ideas about the function and potentialities of the Panchayats which will in the long run be foundation of the Praja Parishad (Subject's Council), the constitution of which are going to announce today. With the experience gained by the Panchayats it is our earnest desire to form local bodies of bigger administrative units e.g. Praja Sava in each Tehsil namely sadar, Ratnaprava, Bhagirathpur, Surapratap Pur, Raisinghaprasad and Parjang which will supervise and coordinate the activities of the village panchayats and will be the source from which experienced and able members will be returned to the Praja Parishad. The Praja Parishad will comprise of 26 members of whom not less than 50% shall be elected. A member of our state council will be the President of the Parishad and a Deputy President will be appointed by us from among the responsible officers of the state. This institution, representative as it will be in its character, will be helpful to us in studying public opinion on all questions of social and economic importance, will serve a very useful purpose in bringing to the notice of the state administration, the wishes and aspirations of the people and in influencing its course of action in all matters of importance or of material interest to the state and to base our decision thereon. The Parishad will be summoned from time to time as necessity will rise and we desire that it will meet at least twice a year.

The evolution of this process would naturally take time. We have decided to set up in the meantime a Praja Parisad with 26 nominated members from all over the state. It is however our considered opinion that no important interest of our state will remain unrepresented.

The Village Panchayat Act and Rules and Regulations for the Praja Parishad are under preparation and will be issued as soon as they are ready. We have also in mind the improvement in the organization and personnel of the high court which already exists with the addition of a new judge of unimpeachable integrity.

We are further pleased to announce the establishment of a town Municipality in the Dhenkanal town. Municipalities are institutions which must in the first place be properly consolidated and efficiently than before other liberal institutions can prosper. The Dhenkanal Town Municipality will have 12 commissioners: half of whom will be elected and half nominated with one Vice Chairman nominated by us. The town is to be divided into 6 wards each returning one elected member.

The material progress of the people committed to our charge has always been our careful concern and as time proceeds and experience is gained, we shall take further steps towards the realization of this objective. We do hereby announce that the major portion of the state's income will be allocated to administrative charges (which at present is nearly 70% of the total income) and will be spent in the nation building departments such as education, sanitation, agriculture and industry.

In inaugurating the measures indicated above, we assure our beloved subjects with all the emphasis we can command that we are in all sincerity introducing such measures of progress as we believe to be in their best interests under existing conditions. We appeal to all to accept the reforms and privileges announced with a full sense of responsibility and we firmly believe that the sincerity behind the present declaration will evoke an equally sincere response from our beloved people and they will take them in the same spirit of goodwill in which they are granted and give the reforms announced fair and adequate trial without hampering their path of progress by any artificial opposition engendered in any quarter.

We repeat that we grant reforms in all seriousness. No scheme can be perfect at its inception and we fully believe that the reforms announced will make for the ordered progress of the state.

This is our earnest prayer to the Almighty that the reforms introduced today may have his choicest blessings. The Raja and Rayat in the ancient state may henceforth by his grace join hands in a new spirit of cooperation and goodwill and restore to it by their united efforts its pristine glory.- no longer the glory of a conquering military state as in the olden times, but the abiding glory of peace, prosperity and contentment achieved by a well organized and efficiently administered state where traditional Indian culture harmonizes with the progressive modern ideas and where the goodwill of the people forms the bull work of the administration.

Sd/
S.P.S.D.M Bahadur

Annexure-III

Sd/ SP SinghDeo
26-6-1939

Proclamation of
Raja Sri Sri 108 Sri Sankar Pratap Singh Deo
Mahindra Bahadur Vidasagar
Ruler of the State of Dhenkanal
Dated the 26th June 1939

Whereas it is expedient to bring the people of the state into closer association with the administration and to create in them an active interest for the management of their local affairs and to afford them wider facilities for acquainting the administrative authorities with their wishes and aspirations on all important matters affecting their general interest and welfare and with that end in view to constitute representative organizations in the state it is with the most sincere feelings of pleasure that we make the following declarations:-

Firstly:- Establishment of panchayats in villages or groups of villages composed of such number of members as may be prescribed in this behalf by the State and elected by the adult male subjects of the area concerned with Srihpancha nominated by us for administration of local affairs i.e. education, public health and sanitation, irrigation and water supply, agriculture and communication.

Secondly:- Establishment of local bodies to be termed Praja Sabhas in each of 6 tehsils namely Bhagirathapur, Ratnaprava, Surapratapur, Raisighprasad, Sadar and Parjang; 50% of the members of each of the Sabhas will be drawn through indirect election from amongst the members of village panchayats and the remaining 50% and a Chairman will be nominated by the state. These sabhas will exercise supervision over and will coordinate the activities of the village panchayats

Thirdly: Establishment of central representative body designated as Praja Parishad composed of 26 members, not less than 50% of whom shall be elected by the members of Tehsil Praja sabhas and the remaining seats will be filled up by nomination and the president of the Praja Parishad will be appointed by the state from amongst the members of the Executive council and the Deputy President from amongst some of the responsible Officers of the state. As the evolution of this process will naturally take time, all the 26 seats will be filled up by nomination for the present. The function of this body shall be advisory in its nature and it will bring to the state administration, the wishes and aspirations of the people so that its course of action will be influenced in all matters of importance and directed towards the promotion of general interest and welfare of our beloved subjects. It will be called from time to time as necessity arises and it is our desire that it will meet at least twice a year.

Fourthly: Establishment of Municipality in the town of Dhenkanal with 12 commissioners, 6 of whom will be elected by the rate of payers and 6 will be nominated by the state. The Chairman and Vice Chairman of the municipality will be appointed by the authorities. For the purpose of elections the town will be divided into 6 wards, each returning one commissioner.

Fifthly: Whereas it is expedient to create an atmosphere of goodwill and co-operation for the successful working of the reforms already announced we further declare that a remission of 6 months is granted to all prisoners undergoing imprisonment in the state jails and direct withdrawal of all proceedings under section 17 of the Criminal Law Amendment Act.

Sixthly: We announce the allocation of the major portion of our State revenue- not less than 70% of the income for the administrative charges of the state.

Annexure-4

Constitution of Village Panchayat or Union (Some General and Knowledgeable Topics)

Keeping view on the welfare of the citizens, Darbar Sahib has announced the constitution of panchyat, tehsil union and citizen forum (Prajaa Parishad). The purpose of this action is to involve citizens with the state's governance. To operationalize the same announcement, Darbar Sahib has enforced rural people's representation act from the last *suniya*. Village panchayat is the primary institution of self-governance. This is the most important educational center for general public to take the responsibility of state's governance. This law in enacted with an objective of these unions and panchayats to aid in doing immense welfare of the people.

All the villages in the state are divided into 329 panchayats or village-unions. The niji-garh (fort of the king) is not included in this list because an immediate arrangement is being made to establish a municipality. A special union is constituted for villages with more than seven hundred population. Some small villages are also grouped into a union. Based on the population proportion, it is decided that each union will have five to eleven members. A seat is being reserved for a scheduled cast in every union. But two seats are reserved for scheduled cast people in places like Sourak and Palasuni. Male above the age of twenty one without any mental ailment are eligible to vote for members of the Panchayat election. But following are the qualifications required to be eligible for Panchayat member:

· Ability to read and write in Odiya

· Must not be paying taxes less than one rupee or levy of four *anaa*

· Must not a leprosy patient

· Must not have been in jail for two or more years

It is mandatory for one member to return to the panchayat from a village with hundred or more population. No two members can come from a household to a panchayat nor can a person become member in more than one panchayat. These are principal rules for election. Votes will be casted by raising hands in the presence of vote collecting employees. A lottery will be held for places where the members get equal votes. Complaints if any, about the elections can be raised to the collector through the tehsildar within fifteen days. The minister for self- governance minister will make the final decision.

Panchayat can decide about health, irrigation, roads, free forest land, plantation on state's land, development of agriculture and animal husbandry, and cottage industry. Enough power is also given to them on this matter. Government will give funds to each panchayat. Ascertaining local requirements, the panchayat, if they wish can raise subscriptions. Panchayat can also decide on criminal cases related to brawls, defamation, losses, abuses and matters related to kine house. They can also judge small civil cases of money lending. All collections from penalty levied by panchayat shall be deposited in panchayat fund. An odiya translation of this People's representation act has also been published. A copy shall be given to every village free of cost after the publication. Sooner the state employees will be sent to conduct elections in different places. All those who are eligible for casting their vote as per the gazette will be present as per the specified time and place. Those who are desirous of becoming a member of the panchayat can apply near the employees of the state. They will mention following in their application (a) education (b) age (c) how much tax or levy he is paying (d) whether suffering from leprosy or not (e) whether imprisoned for two or more years.

All these matters will be filled in printed forms and such printed forms will be available from the election officers. Deliberately if any matter is misrepresented in this form, the same shall invite criminal cases.

Prince Sri Sri Sesha Pratap Singh Deo
Judicial Minister, Dhenkanal
Dated 20/09/1940

Constitution of Gram Panchayat List, Parajang Circle

Sl. No	Name of the Union or Panchayat	Names of villages under the union or panchayat	No of Members	Name of the election officer	Date of election	Time of election	Comments
1	2	3	4	5	6	7	
1	Gada Palasuni	Gada Palasuni*	6	Sri Raj Kishore Pattanaik Head Master, E T school	3/10/40	Forenoon	
2	Jaradaa	*Dehuri Hada * Jaradaa Karadaa Khaman Dangaa Paala Andhaari	6	Ejana**	Ejana	Afternoon	
3	Toradaanali	*Jhili *Toradaanali	6	Ejana	4/10/40	Afternoon	
4	Mahabir Road	*Mahabir Road	6	Ejana	5/10/40	Forenoon	
5	Kuturia	*Kuturia	6	Ajij Khan Excise M.E.	3/10/40	Forenoon	

162 | Autobiography of Queen Ratnaprava Devi

6	Madaranga Munda	Tipei Jharan *Gola Gadia *Madaranga Munda	6	Ejana	ejana	Afternoon
7	Doliyaa	*Baama *Dolia Gobari	5	Ejana	4/10/40	Forenoon
8	Pathargarh	*PakatMunda *Pathargarh	5	Ejana	5/10/40	Forenoon
9	Chandpur	*Chandpur	6	Sir Chintamani Das Head: Administration	3/10/40	Forenoon
10	Gurujanguli	*Gurujanguli *Jangu	6	Ejana	Ejana	Afternoon
11	Dashipur	*Dashipur	6	Ejana	4/10/40	Forenoon
12	Panga Kira	*Pangakira	6	Ejana	5/10/40	Forenoon
13	Bhejia	*Bhejia Jamunali, Sundar, Munda, Ragaragaa, Bauti naali	6	Sir Maheswar Mishra Chandpur Police Officer	3/10/40	Forenoon
14	Biribolei	*Biribolei	6	Ejana	3/10/40	Afternoon

15	Ghagharmunda	Gadharei *Solagaon *Ghagharmunda *Katumunda Khairaamunda	5	Ejana	4/10/40	Afternoon
16	Asanabahali	Brahmanjhara Asanbahali Khadaa Kendumunda	5	Ejana	5/10/40	Afternoon
17	Basulei	*Basulei	5	Sri Prabhakar Mishra Special Magistrate	3/10/40	Forenoon
18	Kulei	*Kulei Bawanrapala	5	Ejana	ejana	Afternoon
19	Gengutia	Mahanpasi *Rengthali *Raghunathpur Jharanabahali Do muhaani	8	Ejana	4/10/40	Forenoon
20	Manikamaraa	Manikamaraa	6	Ejana	5/10/40	Forenoon

21	SaraKishore Pal	Baadapadaa Patuabili Sarakishora pala Jakaa	6	Ejana	ejana	Afternoon
22	Khaalapaala	*Khaalapaala	6	Prafulla Chandra Mohapatra High school teacher	3/10/40	Forenoon
23	Saraanga	*Saraanga	6	Ejana	3/10/40	Afternoon
24	Jatiaa	*Jatiaa	5	Ejana	4/10/40	Forenoon
25	Damola	*Damola	5	Prafulla Chandra Mohapatra High school teacher	4/10/40	Afternoon
26	Kandarasinghaa	*Kandarsinghaa	8	Ejana	5/10/40	Forenoon
27	Gada Parjanga	*Gada Parjanga	7	Gopinaath Maharana Police officer	3/10/40	Ejana
28	Dihadola	*Singidaa	7	Ejana	3/10/40	Afternoon

29	Gehleikateni	Naranpadaa Diha Dola Hatiluchaani Saalapadaa *Brahmanbedia *Odasingha Gaudaakateni *Pitaahi *Gahlei Kateni	6	Ejana	4/10/40	Forenoon
30	Mundeila	Mundeila *Balabhadrapur *Naupala	6	Ejana	ejana	Afternoon
31	Kuala	*Kuala	8	Ejana	5/10/40	Forenoon
32	Ambapalaasha	*Ambapalaasha *Purunadiha	6	Sir Narahari Das High school teacher	3/10/40	Forenoon
33	Kankadaajodaa	*Kankadaajodaa	6	Ejana	Ejana	Afternoon
34	Kaladaa	*Kaladaa Kundhei Khaala	6	Ejana	4/10/40	Forenoon
35	Jahnaapada	*Jahnaapada *Khandualmunda *Kataraapadaa	8	Ejana	5/10/40	Forenoon

36	Kantora	*Baarabaanka Palikateni *Kantora	6	Sir Jatindra Nath Sircar Postal Inspector	3/10/40	Forenoon
37	Chandpur	*Chandpur	5	Sir Jatindra Nath Sircar Postal Inspector	3/10/40	Afternoon
38	Barihaapur	*Barihapur	9	Ejana	4/10/40	Forenoon
39	Badajharaa	*Badajharaa *Jautukapasi	8	Ejana	5/10/40	Forenoon
40	Mendhapadaa	*Mendhapadaa	6	Sir Nilamani Nanda Head teacher M.E. School	3/10/40	Forenoon
41	Paatarpadaa	*Paatarapadaa	6	Ejana	3/10/40	Afternoon
42	Lodhani	*Lodhani	6	Ejana	4/10/40	Forenoon
43	Paalsaahi	*Saanakamara *Paalasahi	5	Ejana	3/10/40	Afternoon
44	Badakamara	*Badakamara *Goila *Kundanbeipur	6	Ejana	5/10/40	Forenoon

				Sir Ajaati Baral Tehsildaar		
45	Kankilee	*Kankilee	6		3/10/40	Forenoon
46	Basoi	*Basoi	8	Ejana	4/10/40	Forenoon
47	Anlakataa	*Ria *Anlakataa	5	Ejana	5/10/40	Forenoon
48	Kata Bahala	*Kata Bahala	5	Ejana	5/10/40	Afternoon

Foot Note:

*mark villages have population of 100 or more

Casting of votes in the maujaa mentioned in column-2 shall be held in school building, cooperative housing or any convenient plavce of the village

*Ejana** means same*

Pandit Sri Jaya Krushna Mishra

Publicity Officer, Dhenkanal Estate

Annexure- V

Dhenkanal State Gazette
PUBLISHED BY AUTHORITY
Extraordinary
Dhenkanal, 20th September 1940
Declaration of the Court on the Auspices of Sunia

Court held on 13/09/40 on the occasion of Sunia made following declarations:

With intent to transfer the management of education in the hands of citizen representatives in the future, an education board with government and private members will be constituted.

1. Rural Panchayat Law is implemented from the day of suniya in the state and as per this law, elections will be held automatically. An Odiya edition of the law will be published soon.
2. From the day of suniya, citizens will pay for the first six months or any fraction of that, an amount of Rs.6.25 and for the second six months or a fraction there of an amount of Rs 6/ totaling to Rs.12 as penalty for pending taxes. By this decision, the annual penalty of Rs 18/ levied so far has been reduced by Rs. 6/.
3. As per the court order dated 24/9/38, considering the total interest accumulated till the odiya year 1344 amounting to Rs 18000/ of tax is exempted. Matter

of Palashuni is under consideration and shall be announced at appropriate time.

4   (a) A forest advisory board shall be constituted to involve citizens in the management of forests on the mutual interest of government and citizens. A declaration on this matter shall be made in future. (b)During the ruling of the court, any citizen who is penalized above Rs 750/ for any forest related case, if appeals to the court within fifteen days of suniya, the same complaint shall be considered affirmatively. Pandit Sri Jaya Krushna Mishra

Publicity Officer/
Dhenkanal Estate

Foot Note: *Sunia is Bhadav month Shukla Pakhya Dwadasi day. This is the beginning of Odiya year and Puri king's calendar setting day)*

Annexure-6

Notes Written by Raja Shankar Pratap Singh Deo Mahindra Bahadur in 1939

Notes:

<u>No Confidence</u>
1   Inspite of my pledge in my letter that I shall cooperate with K.B, confirmed again in Seraikela, I was confronted with the question if I will cooperate with K.B. by the resident in Calcutta and again at Puri.
2   My nominee for Steno Typist was rejected
3   Letter Pass from Pol. Orissa to KP C/O Post Master Cuttack

<u>Difficult to Rehabilitate</u>
1   My proposal for an enquiry by two High Court Judges rejected
2   Vehement propaganda against me from the agitators
3   The Enquiry Committee Book
4   Blind belief of P.D. to whatever is said
5   Paper impressions
6   Borsteads enquiry is not comprehensive

<u>Health</u>
1   Present state of affairs need a ruler constantly touring in the state. My health doesn't permit me to stay long in the climate

Charm
1. No Children
2. No hope for children
3. Deed of adoption disallowed
4. No desire

My Desire

1. Like to lead a secluded life and keep completely aloof from politics
2. Will be satisfied if only a a pension of Rs 3000/ a month is provided to my wife
3. Do not want anting for myself
4. Allowances of my mother and grand mother to remain intact
5. State to complete the education of the two younger brothers

Merits of My Leaving

1. Congress and the state people organization will be happy
2. Govt. may reshuffle the administration as they like
3. Get rid of any officer they like
4. Take of Khanja and Lakharaj
5. Reduce a lot of expenditure

My Pledge

1. I shall remain always loyal to the crown
2. Though I shall leave the state I shall be too pleased to go into the army at any time I am sent for
3. Prepared to stay even in a place in front of the nose of a political officer

Prayer
1. I had given a pledge to Col Robson to stay on a year and bring the state into normal condition which I have done
2. Due to bad health can not stay under the present circumstances
3. If no reply is received within.... I shall leave the state empowering the CM who is Govt. Nominee to run the state
4. If there is any restriction that I can not leave the state without naming my successor in the absence of an heir appranet my first choice is Rajkumar S P singhDeo who has worked here as a Dostrict Magistrate for a year, sessions judge for a year, High Curt judge for two years, and has held charges in all different branches of administration. He is popular, well educated and is the second brther. The next choice is on the 4th Rajkumar G P Singh Deo who is undergoing a course in LLB and Bar-at-Law in England and is an intellgient boy without any vices.
5. Paramount power is the custodian of our ijjat (respect) and integrity and if I can not maintain my ijjat and self respect I can not possible convince myself to stay on. How ijjat has been affected?
6. Correspondence from POl Orissa carried through Cuttack post office C/O Post Master. This has given rise to the conclusion that the Political Department has no confidence on me. It would have been more honourable to have asked ne to go out that to treat me like a criminal and insult and humiliate me before my people. The action itself will make my position more difficult yo take ups the responsibility of administration.

7	Deviation from the prescribed procedure of letters from Post Office
8	Letters received by the CM are sealed letters to me
9	Replies are sent independently of me and subsequently I will have to stand by those promises though they are not told to me.

Annexure-VII

On the pious day of Jishu's birth
Sweetness around in the year;
Wishing this in the feet of God
Being highly conscious
Spend life in eternal bliss.

Keeping father's ideology in front
Walk on the path of Karma upwardly;
The valiant Rajput
Keep a grateful and pious life
Shine the earth with knowledge

Annexure -VIII

Death of His Excellency King of Dhenkanal
(Death Due to Heart Attack)
(Published in the Samaj, Dated 4/8/65)
Bhubaneswar 3/8: The Swatantra Party Members of Rajya Sabhaa (Upper House), The king of Dhenkanal Sri Shankar Pratap Singh Deo Mahindra Bahadur passed away today morning in his Kolkata residence. He died due to heart attack. He was sixty one year old at the time of death. His wife Mrs. Ratna Prabha Devi is a member of Odisha Legislative Assembly and has two sons. (P.T.)

(Dead body was brought to Bhubaneswar)
(Published in Samaj Dated 7/8/65)
After the demise of King Sahib of Dhenkanal at Kolkata, his dead body was brought to Bhubaneswar today afternoon in the West Bengal Government's airplane. It is in the news that the same will be taken to Dhenkanal for cremation.

It is a matter of sorrow that India's upper house member, the king of Dhenkanal had suddenly passed away. He was also a member of Odisha assembly for few years. The queen of Dhenkanal is a member from the beginning of the elections. Dhenkanal has come to limelight for various reasons. Late King Shankar Pratap's father late King Sura Pratap was an ideal king. At a time when there were rarely schools in the British ruled Odisha, he had established a high school in Dhenkanal by recruiting very high quality teachers to promote education. Many reputed and highly educated people of Odisha studied in this school and many of them are still working in different spheres of life with high reputation. On his demise, the state was put under court of wards before being ruled by King Shankar Pratap. Of course, he was highly educated

Shankar Pratap Singh Deo
(Hindusthan Standard, August 9th)

In the premature death of Rja Bahadur Sankar Pratap Singh Deo of Dhenkanal, Orissa loses one of the state's most popular leaders. He was only 62 years of age at the time of his death. Sankar Pratap was a Swatantra party member of the Rajya Sabha from Orissa. Well known for his large charities, the Raja Bahadur was of a religious bent of mind and took particular interest in the upkeep and maintenance of the ancient temples and monuments at Dhenkanal, which have fallen on evil days recently. He also took a keen interest in the spread of education and under his rulership even before its integration, Dhenkanal become one of the most advanced states of Orissa.

Born on November 15, 1904, Sankar Pratap was educated at Rajkumar College Raipur and Ravenshaw College, Cuttack. He was for some time a pupil of Late Sri Jadunath Sarkar and the late Mr Prafulla Sarkar, former editor, Anand Bazar Patrika. Mr Janaki nath Bose, father of Netaji Subhash Chandra Bose was his guardian while he was a student in Cuttack. The training he received from those eminent personalities was to great extent responsible in molding his character and for his enlightened outlook in his mature years. Sankar Pratap was a member of the Orissa Legislative Assembly from 1957 to 1962. He became a member of the Rajya Sabha in 1964. A life member of the Calcutta Club, Calcutta Kenel Club and A.A.E.I, he was a sportsman of repute and a kin shikari (hunter). He was a member of the National Rifle Association. He was also connected with the Magic Circle (London) and was a fellow of Royal Society of Arts. The title 'Vidyasagar' was conferred on him by the Benaras Pandit Sabha. A much travelled man, he visited the America, the UK and the continent twice. He visited the Netherlands as the leader of the Indian Contingent of Boys Scouts at the world Jamboree. Entire Orissa Share the grief at his death with his wife and children.

Dr Harekrishna Mehtab

36 Canning Lane
New Delhi
Date 06-08-1965

Respected Queen Sahibaa

Being disturbed and after dealiberating a lot on whether I should write to you or not and what to write- I am writing this letter to you with a heavy heart. I received the sad demise of the king sahib on 3rd. I met him in Delhi on that day- he was fit and fine. He was joking as usual. There was no indication that he would depart so early. I had acquaintance with him from 1938. Despite so many issues, mishapennings and unfrtnate situations, our cordinal relationship was never interrupted. I am deeply saddened by his death.

What consolation can I give you? I didn't like to send a routine and formal letter or telegram of condolence to you. What kind of consolation can I give you suddenly? You are a sharp, intelligent and judicious lady. You could be seeing the hand of God on every act and incident Man is like a machine run by invisible power. Happiness and sorrow is only a guise for him. The almighty will bestow peace to your new king sahib. May the sould rest in peace

(Harekrishna Mehtab)

In Memory of Father

Shri Matru Prasad Singh Deo

It is a year since father's demise. He is always in my memory and life is perturbed in his absence.

We have been able to build our life based on the advice he has given us over last twenty h of three years. He was so abundnant with his affection that he used to take us wherever he was travelling. As a result of this, we could see many places as well as meet many people. Though he used to get angry on our mischiefs but in fewer than later moments he would share funny things to reduce our pain. If he could find out that we are not satisfied with his fuuny words, he would make us to visit many places and even if we were still not happy, he would give us foods of our liking. He would never hit his children and only counsel them with his words. Its not only on studies, but he would train us in book binding, cooking and gardening. He would advise us on how to be cordinal and maganminus towards people. His intention was also to make other children studious and gentleman along with us. His main purpose of advice for all was to lead a simple lving without showing off the abundance.

He tried to acquire knowledge while studying at Rajkumar College in Raipur. Despite being a king, he acquired knowledge by reading books. He always had interest on defence, police, scouting, sports and exercises. Starting from science, he *had knowledge and interest on animal rearing, carepentry, mechanical work and agriculture. He was motivating others to be as knowledgeable on all subjects as himself.*

Many a times, people were dissatisfied with him without understanding his intentions. Even there were citizen issues during his time. After knowing his love, affection and qualities, the citizens had shown him love and respect. Even after losing administrative power, people had elected him as a member to the legislative assembly.

His thoughts were about always about overall wellbeing of people of Dhenkanal and how they can earn reputation and have a sense of pride. Everyone will remember him for this.

I am saddened by that fact that I lost him during my childhood days. I wont get his affection and I lost the opportunity to learn whatever I could from him.

Annexure-IX

Viceroy's Agent
By
Charles Chenevix Trench
(Page No 288 & 289)

The King of Dhenkanal was to be arrested at the first news of a Japanese landing. Biscoe found him an unlovable character, stepped in drugs and drinks, a known supporter of Congress. But Hancock, with hindsight was inclined to think that the Rajah misjudged. The fact that he was a member of the Magic Circle who mystified cultivators by producing rupees are of their ears made me very uneasy.

Some ass in Delhi issued an order that, in the event of invasion, all Political should stay put and collaborate with the enemy to keep essential services running; this despite evidence from Malaya and Burma that the enemy had no intention of collaborating with any British Officials, only of beheading them or locking them up. Hancock treated this order with the contempt it deserved. He would, he informed Delhi, to take to the jungle with as many armed police and aboriginal bowmen as he could muster and harass the enemy until he was scuppered. Michel (recently in South Waziristan) went one better. There were in the area many pathan traders and money lenders, no strangers to guerrilla was and very willing to form guerilla bands provided the

Government gave them rifles and hand grenades. With this proposal Mitchel and Biscoe went to the Resident.

His receipt of my message was enthusiastic. His only criticism was that I had not proposed a scale of blood money graduated to the rank and importance of our victims...Biscoe was sent in his official car, Union Jack fluttering, to the fort of Calcutta to indent for our weaponry and arrange for its delivery.

The Japanese were held in Burma, their raids on Colombo were defeated and their aircraft carriers withdrew from the Bay of Bengal. The danger of Japanese invasion receded; But a new peril loomed.

When Britain declared war on Japan, Nehru's first reaction was to be proud at least for being British. He, Ballav Bhai Patel and Other Congress Leaders would have cooperated against an enemy far more a threat to Indian than Germany was. But Gandhi called them to heel. In obstruction and disruption and generally negative measures he had no match: it was only when constructive policies were required that his shortcomings became apparent. He scorned the British Government's offer of Dominion status immediately after the war, a postdated cheque on a failing bank and demanded that Britain immediately 'Quit India'. He envisaged an easy Japanese victory, followed by Japan handing over India to Indians- or- rather to Congress. If the Japanese seemed disposed to stay, they could be removed by love and soul force. Since the British didn't seem willing to oblige him, he (with the other congress leaders in dutiful chorus) launched a campaign of open opposition to the war efforts. It would, of course be 'non-violent' (In the Mahatma's view blowing up small railway bridges was not violent). Like a long awaited bush fire, the rebellion blazed through the United, Central, Bihar and Orissa Province and the Eastern States.

Railways were one of the main targets. Stations were destroyed, signal boxes put out of action, rails torn up. For three weeks rail communication between Delhi and Calcutta was cut off. There were some shocking murders of railway staff. Two Canadian Air Force Officers in an immobilized train were induced to give up their revolvers and the hauled out of the train and beaten to death.

An R.A.F place, patrolling the line was compelled to ditch in a river: as the crew swarm ashore, villagers pushed them under with Ples. Biscoe saw the sequel.

In found myself in a small state where a mob was programmed to meet next morning and march on the palace. I was able to wire Calcutta where Colonel Hancock alerted the R.A.F. A mob did indeed assemble in a large mango grove. While no attack was reported the air gunners did, as was customary, test their guns after they were air borne. By some sort of coincidence a number of men in the mob were wounded and the mob broke up. This was just as well we could have mistered only a total of nine rifles among us if the need has arisen.

After railways, police stations and district offices were attacked. The police were amazingly true to their salt; Nitchell heard of no cases of them surrendering, although if they were overwhelmed, as was often the case, they were burnt to death.

The first of the Orissa States to be hit by the rebellion was Talcher (Non saulte). A mob tried to burn down the palace. The Rajah, a stout –hearted young man, ordered his twenty policemen to charge the insurgents and arrest the lot. This they did, but the jail superintendent refused to admit 2000 prisoners to a jail built for forty.

Hancock arrived for consultations.

BLACK EAGLE BOOKS

www.blackeaglebooks.org
info@blackeaglebooks.org

Black Eagle Books, an independent publisher, was founded as a nonprofit organization in April, 2019. It is our mission to connect and engage the Indian diaspora and the world at large with the best of works of world literature published on a collaborative platform, with special emphasis on foregrounding Contemporary Classics and New Writing.